A QUICK COURSE IN

WORDPERFECT® 6

For Windows

POLLY URBAN

JOYCE COX

PUBLISHED BY
Online Press Incorporated
14320 NE 21st Street, Suite 18
Bellevue, WA 98007
(206) 641-3434, (800) 854-3344

Publisher's Cataloging in Publication
(Prepared by Quality Books Inc.)

    Urban, Polly.
      A quick course in WordPerfect 6 for Windows / Polly Urban, Joyce
Cox.
      p. cm.
      Includes index.
      ISBN 1-879399-30-X

      1. WordPerfect for Windows (Computer file)   2. Word processing.
    I. Cox, Joyce.   II. Title.

    Z52.5.W65F676 1993   652.5'536
                              QBI93-21967
                                        93-086379
                                        CIP

Printed and bound in the United States of America

2 3 4 5 6 7 8 9 W P W N 3 2 1 0

Acknowledgment
Many thanks to Dr. Kaye Fox, WordPerfect guru and father extraordinaire, for laying the foundation on which this book is built.

Other Quick Course® books
Don't miss our other Quick Course® titles!

A Quick Course in Windows 3.1 • *A Quick Course in Windows for Workgroups*
A Quick Course in Paradox for Windows • *A Quick Course in Quattro Pro for Windows*
A Quick Course in DOS 6 • *A Quick Course in WordPerfect 6 for DOS*
A Quick Course in Excel for Windows • *A Quick Course in Lotus 1-2-3 Release 4 for Windows*
• *A Quick Course in Word for Windows*
Plus many more. Call us at 1-800-854-3344

Contents

1

First Things First

What you will learn

You're probably sitting at your computer with the DOS prompt (C:\>) on your screen. More than likely, you have letters and reports to write, and you're anxious to get started with WordPerfect for Windows. But first, those of you who have never used WordPerfect for Windows before need to cover some basics, such as how to get around WordPerfect's document window, select parts of a document, give instructions, save and open documents, and back up files. In this chapter, we also review some Windows techniques, but we assume you've already used Windows enough to be familiar with basic operations. (If you are new to Windows as well as new to WordPerfect for Windows, we suggest you take a look at *A Quick Course in Windows*, another book in the Quick Course series.) After you learn a few fundamentals, you'll easily be able to create the documents we cover in the rest of the book.

If you are already familiar with WordPerfect 5.1 or 5.2 for Windows, this book brings you quickly up to speed with WordPerfect 6 for Windows. You can skim this chapter for information about new and improved features, and then get down to work with Chapter 2.

Getting Started

We assume that you've already installed both Windows and WordPerfect 6 for Windows on your computer, and that you're ready to go. (We don't give detailed instructions for installing the program because WordPerfect guides you through the process.) We also assume you're using a mouse. Although it is possible to work with WordPerfect for Windows using only the keyboard, the Windows environment is tailor-made for point-and-click mouse techniques, and using a mouse with WordPerfect for Windows is both intuitive and efficient.

The simplest way to start WordPerfect for Windows is from the Windows Program Manager. Follow these steps:

1. Type *win* at the C:\> prompt, and press Enter.

   Starting Windows

2. If necessary, double-click the WPWin 6.0 group icon to open the WPWin 6.0 group window.

3. In the group window, double-click the WPWin 6.0 icon to start the program. WordPerfect's copyright screen makes a brief appearance, and a few seconds later, you see this document window:

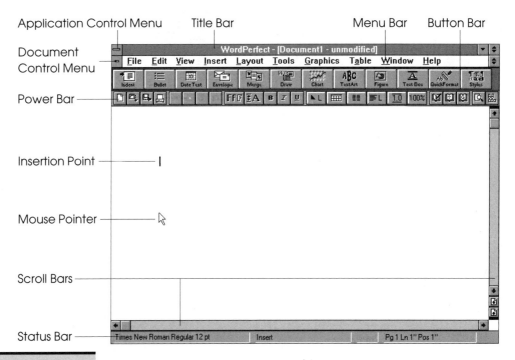

Using the scroll bars

The document window is often not big enough to display all of its contents. To bring out-of-sight information into view, you use the scroll bars. Clicking the arrow at the end of a scroll bar moves the window's contents a small distance in the direction of the arrow. Clicking on either side of a scroll box (both of which are now at the ends of their scroll bars) moves the contents one windowful. The position of the scroll box in relation to the scroll bar indicates the position of the window in relation to its contents. Drag the scroll box to see specific parts of a document; for example, the middle or end.

At the top of the window, the *title bar* tells you that you are looking at Document1 and that you have not yet modified the document. As soon as you type something or choose a command, *unmodified* will disappear, letting you know that the document has changed since you last saved it. Below the title bar is a *menu bar* from which you choose commands. (We discuss choosing commands on page 6.) Next comes the *Button Bar* and the *Power Bar*, which give you point-and-click access to WordPerfect's most frequently used commands. Across the bottom of the window is the *status bar*, which is divided into areas called *fields*. In the left field, WordPerfect displays the currently selected font. (We discuss fonts on page 57.) *Insert* tells you that any characters you type will be inserted in the document; *Pg* tells you which page you are on (in this case, page 1); and *Ln* and *Pos* state your position, in inches, from the top and left margins of the page.

Toward the top-left corner of the blank window sits the *insertion point* (the blinking vertical bar). The insertion point shows you where the action is—where the next character you type will be inserted or which character will be deleted if you press the Delete key. You also see your *mouse pointer*, which is an I-beam when it is over the blank window and a white arrow when it is anywhere else on the screen. The mouse pointer shows the location of the mouse relative to the screen and moves independently of the insertion point.

The mouse pointer

Now let's get down to business. So that you will have a document to work with, type the following note (which we've magnified so that it is easy to read). In case you're new to computers, you use the Shift key to enter capital (uppercase) letters and the Backspace key to erase mistakes. As you type, note the changes in the status bar.

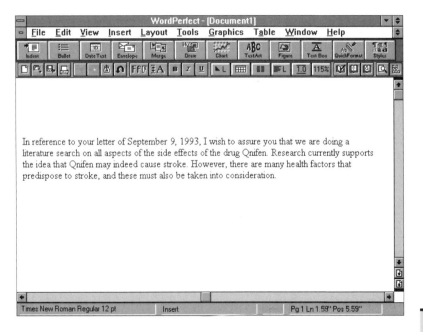

As each line of text reaches the right edge of the screen, the next word you type moves to a new line. This is called *word wrapping*.

Moving Around the Screen

You can move around the screen in a variety of ways. The easiest way is to use your mouse to quickly move the insertion point anywhere in a document. Simply position the I-beam pointer at the desired location, and click the left mouse button.

Starting over

If you make a mistake while creating the note (or any other document in this book) and want to start over in a clear window, simply choose the Close command from the File menu, and then click No when WordPerfect asks whether you want to save the document. (See page 6 if you need help choosing commands.)

Navigating with the mouse

The mouse really shines when you want to move around a document that is longer than the screen. To move to a location that is currently out of view, use the mouse and the scroll bar on the right side of the window to display the desired part of the document on the screen, and then click the mouse button to position the insertion point.

Navigating with the keyboard

You can also use the keyboard to move around. Pressing the Up, Down, Left, and Right Arrow keys moves the insertion point up and down one line and left and right one character. But moving a line or character at a time is not the most efficient way to get around. Here are some faster ways:

To move the insertion point...	Press...
Left one word	Ctrl+Left Arrow
Right one word	Ctrl+Right Arrow
To beginning of line	Home
To beginning of line before codes	Home,Home
To end of line	End
Up one paragraph	Ctrl+Up Arrow
Down one paragraph	Ctrl+Down Arrow
To top of screen (then up a screen)	PgUp
To bottom of screen (then down a screen)	PgDn
Up one page	Alt+PgUp
Down one page	Alt+PgDn
To beginning of document	Ctrl+Home
To beginning of document before codes	Ctrl+Home,Ctrl+Home
To end of document	Ctrl+End

Try using various keys and key combinations to move around the note. When you're reasonably "mobile," rejoin us for a discussion of text selection techniques.

Selecting Text

Knowing how to select text efficiently saves you time because you can then edit and apply formatting to blocks of text, instead of having to deal with individual characters. Follow along as we demonstrate selecting text blocks of different shapes and sizes, first with the mouse:

Keyboard conventions

When two keys are separated by a plus sign, such as Ctrl+Right Arrow, press and hold down the first key, and then press the second key. When two or more keys are separated by commas, such as Ctrl+Home,Ctrl+Home, press and release each key or key combination in the order in which it appears in the instruction.

1. Point to the first word of the note, and double-click the mouse button to select the word and the space after it.

2. Point to the word *currently* in the second sentence, and triple-click the mouse button to select the sentence containing that word.

3. Point to any word, and quadruple-click (click four times) to select the entire paragraph.

4. Move the mouse pointer to the left of the first line of your document, and when the pointer changes to a white arrow, click to select the first sentence, and then double-click to select the paragraph.

You don't have to select discreet units like words, sentences, or paragraphs. If you are skilled with your mouse, you can drag through the text itself to highlight exactly as much or as little as you need. You can also use your mouse in conjunction with the Shift key, like this:

1. Click an insertion point just before the word *we* in the first sentence.

Shift-clicking to
select text

2. Point in front of the period at the end of the sentence, hold down the Shift key, and click the mouse button. As you can see here, WordPerfect highlights all the characters between the two clicks:

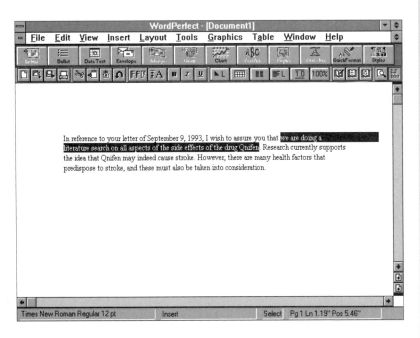

Selecting text with commands

Sometimes you might find it easier to select a specific unit of text by using a command. Choosing Select from the Edit menu displays a submenu from which you can choose Sentence, Paragraph, Page, or All. (The Select All command is particularly useful for selecting all the text in a long document.) If your text includes lists of items that you have created using tabs or indents, you can select a "column" of text by choosing Select and then Tabular Column. You can also select a block of text by choosing Select and then Rectangle.

3. Click anywhere in the note to remove the highlight.

Now let's look at a couple of useful keyboard selection methods:

Select mode

1. Press the F8 key to turn on Select mode. In the status bar, WordPerfect tells you that the mode is active.

2. Press the Right, Left, Up, and Down Arrow keys to select blocks of text of various shapes and sizes.

3. Try using several of the navigation key combinations listed in the table on page 4 in conjunction with Select mode to see their effects.

4. Press F8 again to turn off Select mode.

When Select mode is not turned on, you can use the Shift key with other keys to highlight specific units of text. Here's a list of some of these units and the keys that select them:

To select...	Press...
A character left or right	Shift+Left Arrow or Shift+Right Arrow
A word left or right	Shift+Ctrl+Left Arrow or Shift+Ctrl+Right Arrow
A line up or down	Shift+Up Arrow or Shift+Down Arrow
A paragraph up or down	Shift+Ctrl+Up Arrow or Shift+Ctrl+Down Arrow
A screen up or down	Shift+PgUp or Shift+PgDn
A page up or down	Shift+Alt+PgUp or Shift+Alt+PgDn
To beginning or end of line	Shift+Home or Shift+End
To beginning or end of document	Shift+Ctrl+Home or Shift+Ctrl+End

Giving Instructions

You can give WordPerfect instructions in three ways: using menu commands; using shortcut keys and key combinations; and using buttons on the Button Bar and Power Bar. We'll look briefly at all three methods in this section.

Using Menu Commands

With earlier DOS versions of WordPerfect, you gave most instructions by using various keys and key combinations.

Now the emphasis has shifted away from the keyboard and toward the mouse. Instead of having to remember the key combination for carrying out an action, you can give instructions visually, by choosing commands from menus. Try this:

1. Move the mouse pointer over the word *View* on the menu bar at the top of your screen, and click the left mouse button once to display the View menu. Some of the commands on this menu are preceded by check marks, which indicate that the commands are toggles that can be turned on and off (a checked command is turned on). Others are followed by key combinations, indicating that pressing that key combination activates the command without pulling down the menu. You can close a menu without choosing a command by clicking anywhere outside the menu or by pressing Esc or Alt.

Displaying menus

Closing menus

2. Move the mouse pointer over the Ruler Bar command on the View menu, and click the left mouse button to display WordPerfect's ruler, which you use to set such layout elements as margins, indents, and tabs (see page 110 for more information about the Ruler Bar):

Choosing commands

— Ruler Bar

Choosing commands from the keyboard

From the keyboard, you can press Alt to activate the menu bar and then press the underlined letter of the name of the menu you want to open. To move from one menu to another, use the Left and Right Arrow keys. When you have located the command you want, press its underlined letter to choose it.

3. Click the word *File* on the menu bar. As you can see, some of the File-menu commands are followed by arrowheads. When you choose a command followed by an arrowhead, a

submenu listing more commands appears. You choose a command from a submenu the same way you choose one from a regular menu. Other commands are followed by ellipses. An ellipsis indicates that when you choose the command, a dialog box will appear so that you can give WordPerfect the additional information it needs to carry out the command.

Dialog boxes

4. Choose the Preferences command from the File menu to display the Preferences dialog box:

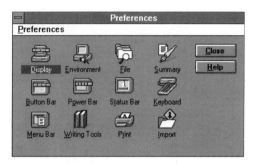

5. To tell WordPerfect what type of preferences you want to work with, double-click the Environment icon. WordPerfect displays the Environment Preferences dialog box:

Edit boxes

In this dialog box, you can type information in an *edit box*; for example, you can enter your name in the Name edit box. You can turn some options on or off by clicking the adjacent *check box* (an X in the box means the option is turned on); for example, you can tell WordPerfect to beep your computer

Check boxes

when an error occurs by clicking the Error check box in the Beep On group box. You can select from a set of options, called a *pop-up option list*, by pointing to the arrows to the right of the option's name, holding down the mouse button, moving the highlight to the desired item, and then releasing the mouse button; for example, you would use this technique to change the Hyphenation Prompt option. You can also select from a set of *mutually exclusive options* by clicking one round button in the set; for example, only one of the options in the Save Workspace group box can be selected at any given time. In the top-right corner of the dialog box are four *command buttons*. Clicking a command button that is followed by an ellipsis displays yet another dialog box with more choices.

Pop-up option lists

Mutually exclusive options

Command buttons

6. Click the Code Page button to display this dialog box:

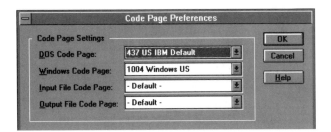

You use the Code Page Preferences options to select a character set when you are importing or exporting documents in

Custom menu bars

You can create custom menu bars and menus so that options you use frequently are easily accessible. Right-click the menu bar, and choose Preferences from the QuickMenu. Then click the Create button, and in the Create Menu Bar dialog box, type a name for the new menu bar, and click OK to display the Menu Bar Editor. Now you can edit the menu bar. Remove a menu you don't need by simply dragging it off the menu bar and releasing the mouse button when you see the trash can icon. Add a menu by dragging the Menu icon in the bottom-right corner of the dialog box to where you want it on the menu bar; double-click the new menu to edit its name. To add features to the new menu, start with the Activate A Feature option selected in the Add A Menu Item To group box. (You can select Play A Keyboard Script, Launch A Program, or Play A Macro to add other types of actions to the menu.) Then select a menu name from the Feature Categories drop-down list, select an item from the Features list, and drag the item to the new menu. When the menu drops down, move the pointer to the location where you want to insert the selected item, and release the mouse button to add the item to the menu. To move an item from one menu to another, pull-down the menu where the item is currently located, and drag the item to the desired location on the new menu. When the menu is complete, click OK, and then click Select to return to your document with the custom menu bar displayed. After you have created a menu bar, you can edit it by selecting it in the Menu Bar Preferences dialog box and clicking Edit to display the Menu Bar Editor; you can't edit the built-in WordPerfect menu bar.

languages other than English. You change each option by clicking the arrow at the right end of its edit box to display a *drop-down list* of possible settings. If the list is longer than the list box, you use the scroll bar to the right of the box to bring more settings into view.

Drop-down lists

7. Click Cancel to close the Code Page Preferences dialog box without changing the existing settings, and then click Cancel to close the Environment Preferences dialog box with the original settings still in effect. (If you wanted to implement any changes you have made in these dialog boxes, you would click OK or press Enter instead of clicking Cancel.)

8. Click Close to close the Preferences dialog box.

You'll practice using all these methods of giving information as we work our way through the book.

Using QuickMenus

QuickMenus group together the commands you are likely to use for an element of a document or window. You access a QuickMenu by pointing to the element and clicking the right mouse button. To see how QuickMenus work, try this:

Right-clicking to display QuickMenus

1. Point to the Ruler Bar, and click the right mouse button once. (From now on, we'll refer to this action as *right-clicking*.) WordPerfect displays the Ruler Bar's QuickMenu, listing all the actions you are most likely to perform with the Ruler Bar.

2. Choose Hide Ruler Bar from the QuickMenu. WordPerfect removes the Ruler Bar from the screen.

Throughout this book, we'll use QuickMenus whenever they are the most efficient way of accomplishing a particular task.

Using Shortcut Key Combinations

With WordPerfect for Windows, you can use Ctrl, Shift, and Alt key combinations to give instructions. Try the following:

1. Hold down Alt+Shift, and press F3 to redisplay the Ruler Bar.

2. Click View in the menu bar. The Ruler Bar toggle command is now preceded by a check mark. Choose the command to turn off the Ruler Bar.

Using the Button Bar and Power Bar

The Button Bar and Power Bar both provide point-and-click ways of carrying out common word-processing tasks with the mouse. Let's look at each of them in turn.

The Button Bar

The buttons on the Button Bar provide instant access to Word-Perfect features that enable you to create professional-looking documents. We will use many of these buttons as we work our way through this book. For now, let's look at a couple of simple examples. To give an instruction using the Button Bar, you click the appropriate button. If WordPerfect needs more information before it can carry out the instruction, it displays a dialog box, just as if you had chosen the corresponding command from a menu. Try this:

1. Press Ctrl+Home to move to the beginning of the note.

2. Click the Date Text button on the Button Bar. WordPerfect inserts the current date at the beginning of the paragraph.

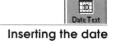

Inserting the date

3. Press Enter to move the text of the note to a new line, leaving the date in a paragraph of its own.

4. With the insertion point at the beginning of the note paragraph, click the Indent button on the Button Bar. WordPerfect indents the text of the note, like this:

Indenting paragraphs

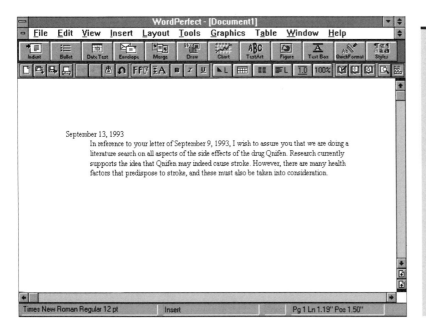

> **Feature bars**
>
> In addition to placing commonly used commands within easy reach on the Button Bars and Power Bar, WordPerfect uses feature bars to provide easy access to the commands you'll use with specific features, such as tables, footnotes, and outlines. When you activate these features, Word-Perfect automatically displays the corresponding feature bar below the Power Bar. We'll work with several different feature bars in the course of this book.

WordPerfect comes with 12 Button Bars, each with a combination of buttons that is most appropriate for a particular kind of task. For example, the Graphics Button Bar contains the buttons you are most likely to need when creating and manipulating graphics. You can also create your own Button Bars by assigning commands to buttons, arranging the buttons on a bar to suit your fancy, and then saving the custom Button Bar for future use. You can display the Button Bar across the top of your screen—the default position—or you can specify that it appear elsewhere. And your buttons can sport pictures, names, or both. Let's experiment:

Changing the Button Bar look and location

1. Point to the Button Bar, right-click the mouse, choose Preferences from the group of commands at the *bottom* of the menu, and then click the Options button to display this dialog box:

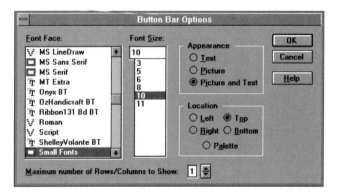

Changing the Button Bar position and shape

The Button Bar is not limited to the four locations specified in the Button Bar Options dialog box. You can drag the Button Bar anywhere in the document window by pointing to the vertical border between two buttons or to a blank area of the bar, holding down the left mouse button, and dragging to the desired location. When you drag anywhere other than to the top, bottom, left, or right edge of the window, the Button Bar changes from a bar to a rectangular palette.

2. Select Text in the Appearance group box and Left in the Location group box, click OK to close the Button Bar Options dialog box, and then click Close to close the Button Bar Preferences dialog box. Here's the result:

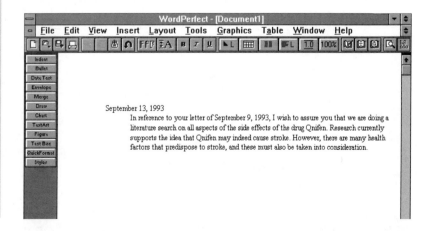

3. Right-click the Button Bar, choose Preferences again, select Options, reset the Appearance setting to Picture And Text and the Location setting to Top, and click OK, leaving the Button Bar Preferences dialog box open.

Now let's add a button to the active Button Bar:

1. In the Available Button Bars list, *WordPerfect* is highlighted to indicate that the default WordPerfect Button Bar is currently active. Without moving the highlight, click the Edit button to display this dialog box:

Adding buttons

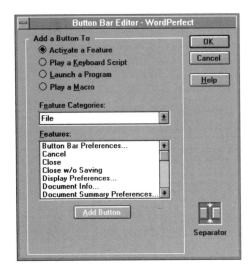

(You can also access this dialog box by right-clicking the Button Bar and choosing Edit from the QuickMenu.) WordPerfect assumes you want to add a feature button, and by default, lists all the features you can access through the File menu. You can select other menus from the Feature Categories drop-down list to display their features.

2. Scroll to the bottom of the Features list box until Template comes into view. (The Template command on the File menu gives you access to a set of predefined WordPerfect files that you can use to quickly generate standard documents; see page 26 for more information.)

3. Point to Template, and hold down the left mouse button. When the button-and-hand icon appears, drag the icon up to the left end of the Button Bar, and release the mouse button. WordPerfect adds a Template button to the Button Bar.

Custom Button Bars

To create a custom Button Bar, right-click the Button Bar, and choose Preferences from the QuickMenu. Then click the Create button, and in the Create Button Bar dialog box, type a name for the new Button Bar, and click OK to display the Button Bar Editor. Now you can assemble your Button Bar. With the Activate A Feature option selected in the Add A Button To group box, select a menu from the Feature Categories drop-down list, select an item from the Features list, and either click Add Button or drag the item to the Button Bar. You can select Play A Keyboard Script, Launch A Program, or Play A Macro to add other types of actions to the Button Bar. When the Button Bar is complete, click OK, and then click Select to return to your document with the custom Button Bar displayed on your screen.

4. With the Button Bar Editor still on your screen, point to the Template button, hold down the mouse button, drag the Template button to the right so that it sits over both the Date Text and the Envelope buttons, and release the mouse button. WordPerfect rearranges the Button Bar, placing the Template button between the Date Text and Envelope buttons.

5. Click OK to close the Button Bar Editor dialog box, and then click Close to close the Button Bar Preferences dialog box. The Button Bar now looks like this:

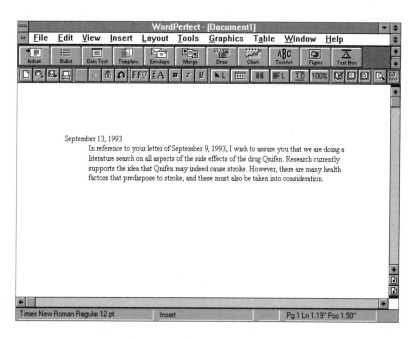

Two buttons, QuickFormat and Styles, may now be out of sight. You can scroll these buttons into view by clicking the arrows at the right end of the Button Bar.

The Power Bar

You use the Power Bar to quickly carry out common file operations and editing and formatting tasks. You can perform these tasks by choosing commands from menus, but clicking buttons and selecting options from the pop-up lists on the Power Bar is usually more efficient. We'll put many Power Bar buttons through their paces in the next chapter.

After you gain more experience with WordPerfect for Windows, you may find that you rarely use some of the buttons or that you often use commands not currently represented by

Deleting buttons and Button Bars

To delete a button from a Button Bar, right-click the Button Bar, and then choose Edit from the QuickMenu. Next, point to the button you want to delete, hold down the left mouse button, and drag the button away from the Button Bar. Release the mouse button when you see the small trash can icon. To delete a Button Bar, right-click the Button Bar, and choose Preferences from the QuickMenu. Highlight the Button Bar you want to delete, click the Delete button, and then click Yes to confirm the deletion.

buttons on the Power Bar. You can change the buttons using techniques similar to those described for the Button Bar. However, you can't change the position of the Power Bar.

Saving Documents

You probably know that the note you have typed and edited currently exists in your computer's memory and that this memory (called *RAM* for *random access memory*) is temporary. All information in RAM is wiped out when you turn off your computer. To move the note to a more permanent storage place, you have to save it.

When you save a document for the first time, WordPerfect asks you to supply a filename. Using up to eight characters, you should try to come up with a name that reflects the contents of the document you're saving. And you should be consistent. For example, you might want to assign similar names to documents connected with the same project so that they are readily identifiable as part of that project. To further identify the contents of a file, you can add a filename extension. The extension must be preceded by a period and can be up to three characters. For example, you might use the extensions LET (for letters) and MEM (for memos). Do not use BAT, COM, and EXE, which are reserved for program files.

Naming files

Enough philosophizing. Let's save the note:

1. With the note displayed on your screen, choose the Save As command from the File menu to display this dialog box:

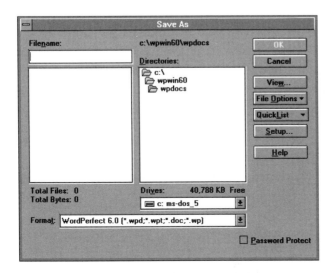

Filename characters

Here's a list of the characters you can use in filenames:

A-Z

0-9

! @ # $ % & ( ) - ' ' _

WordPerfect might accept other characters in filenames or extensions, but sticking with these characters ensures that all your filenames will be valid.

(If the Document Summary dialog box appears before the Save As dialog box, click OK, and then refer to the tip on page 77.)

2. In the Filename edit box, type the filename and the extension (use *qnifen.not* for this example), and press Enter. Word-Perfect saves the file and displays its abbreviated pathname in the title bar at the top of the document window.

After you've saved the document and given it a name, you can click the Save button on the Power Bar or use the Save command on the File menu to save subsequent changes. Choose Save As only if you want to assign a different name to a new version of the document. Don't ever hesitate to use Save. It may *save* your bacon some day.

Backing Up Files

To spare you the trauma of losing work because of machine failures or power outages, or because you somehow managed to make a mess of a document, you should regularly *back up*, or make copies of, your files. While you are creating a document, you can back it up by turning on the Original Document Backup option and then saving the file regularly, or you can have WordPerfect automatically back up your files using its Timed Document Backup option. We discuss both methods in this section.

Retaining the Previous Version of a Document

Each time you save a file, the current version overwrites the previous version. By turning on the Original Document Backup option, you can tell WordPerfect to change the extension of the previous version of the file to BK! so that you can save both the current and previous versions. By default, WordPerfect stores the backup file in the same directory as the current version.

Here's how to activate the Original Document Backup option:

1. Choose the Preferences command from the File menu.

2. Double-click the File icon to display this dialog box:

Pathnames

A file's pathname includes its filename as well as its "address." For example, C:\WPWIN60\-WPDOCS\QNIFEN.NOT tells us that the QNIFEN.NOT file is located in the WPDOCS sub-directory of the WPWIN60 direc-tory, which branches from the main, or root, directory of drive C. By default, WordPerfect saves your documents in the WPDOCS subdirectory. To specify another directory, choose Preferences from the File menu, double-click the File icon, and specify a new location in the Default Directory edit box in the File Preferences dialog box.

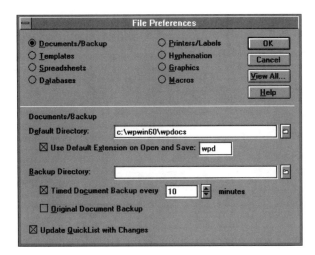

By default, the Documents/Backup option is selected in the top part of the File Preferences dialog box, and its settings are displayed in the lower part. Selecting another option in the top part of the dialog box changes the settings in the lower part to those that are available for the selected option.

3. Click the Original Document Backup check box, and then click OK.

4. Click Close in the Preferences dialog box to return to the document window.

5. Now save QNIFEN.NOT by clicking the Save button on the Power Bar. WordPerfect saves the original file version as QNIFEN.BK!, and the current version as QNIFEN.NOT.

The next time you save QNIFEN.NOT, WordPerfect will delete QNIFEN.BK!, save QNIFEN.NOT as QNIFEN.BK!, and save the new version of the note as QNIFEN.NOT. Then if QNIFEN.NOT is accidentally damaged or deleted, you can retrieve QNIFEN.BK!, rename it QNIFEN.NOT, and reconstruct any changes you have made since the last time you saved the document.

Making Timed Backups

By default, WordPerfect's Timed Document Backup option automatically saves your work every 10 minutes. If you are working with more than one document, WordPerfect creates

Timed backup directory

To store your *timed* backup files in a different directory, type the name of the desired directory in the Backup Directory edit box of the File Preferences dialog box. For example, to store backup files in a special BACKUP directory, enter *c:\wpwin60\backup*. (The BACKUP directory must already exist on your hard drive.)

a backup file for each of them (WP{WPC}.BK1 for document 1, WP{WPC}.BK2 for document 2, and so on). Backup files are stored in the main WordPerfect directory unless you specify another directory. If you lose the current version of your work, through a power outage for example, you can retrieve the backup file and pick up where you left off. WordPerfect deletes these backup files when you end your current work session.

If you decide that 10 minutes is too long an interval between backups, you can change the interval as follows:

1. Choose Preferences from the File menu, and double-click the File icon to display the File Preferences dialog box.

2. In the Timed Document Backup Every edit box, type the desired time interval, and click OK. In the Preferences dialog box, click Close to return to your document.

Opening Documents

To give you some practice in opening existing WordPerfect for Windows documents, let's open the QNIFEN.BK! file that WordPerfect created when you last saved the note. Follow these steps:

1. Click the Open button on the Power Bar to display a dialog box like this one:

Open File

Fil**e**name:
c:\wpwin60\wpdocs   OK

qnifen.bk!   Cancel
qnifen.not
                    Directories: Vie**w**...
                    c:\
                    wpwin60   Quick**F**inder...
                    wpdocs
                                       File **O**ptions ▾

                                       Quick**L**ist ▾

                                       Setup...

                                       Help

Total Files: 2   Dri**v**es: 41,096 KB Free
Total Bytes: 4,504
                        c: ms-dos_5

List Files of **T**ype: All Files (*.*)

File open shortcut

If the file you want to open is one of the four most recently opened files, you can bypass the Open File dialog box and simply choose the file from the bottom of the File menu.

The files listed are stored in the directory specified above the Directories list box. If the file you want is not stored in the current directory, you need to switch to the correct directory in order to select the file. You would double-click C:\ to display the root directory's files and subdirectories; double-click a subdirectory to display its files and subdirectories; and so on.

2. For this example, simply double-click QNIFEN.BK! in the list of filenames. WordPerfect opens the previous version of the note in its own window.

Creating New Documents

You now have two documents open on your screen, though QNIFEN.NOT is totally obscured by QNIFEN.BK!. For good measure, let's open a third document, this time a brand new one. There's just one step:

1. Click the New button on the Power Bar.

That's all there is to it! A new blank document is displayed in a window, on top of QNIFEN.BK! and QNIFEN.NOT.

Manipulating Windows

Now that we have a few windows to play with, we'll pause here to review some window basics. Being able to work with more than one document open at a time is useful, especially if you need to use the same information in different documents. For example, you might use the same text in a memo, a letter, and a legal brief. Follow these steps to see how easy it is to move from one document to another:

1. Click *Window* on the menu bar to display the Window menu, which lists the three open documents.

Activating a document

2. Next choose QNIFEN.NOT from the list of open documents. WordPerfect brings the current version of the memo to the top of the stack of windows.

3. Choose Tile from the Window menu. WordPerfect arranges the three open documents so that they each occupy about a third of the screen, as shown on the next page.

Arranging windows

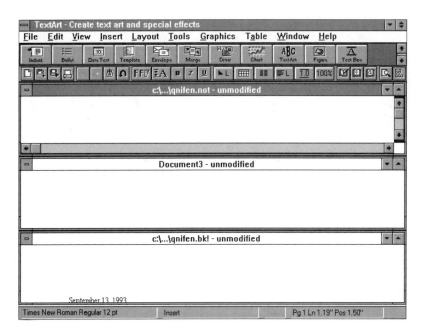

4. Click anywhere in the QNIFEN.BK! window to activate it. Notice that the title bar of the active document is a different color from the other two title bars and that scroll bars appear only in the active window. Any entries you make and any commands you choose will affect only the active document.

5. Click the Maximize button (the upward-pointing arrowhead) in the top-right corner of the QNIFEN.BK! window. The window expands to fill the screen, completely obscuring the other two documents.

Navigating between windows

If your hands are on the keyboard, you can move quickly from one window to another by pressing Ctrl+F6 to move to the window of the next document or pressing Ctrl+Shift+F6 to move to the window of the previous document. (*Next* and *previous* are determined by the order in which the documents were opened.)

6. Click the Open button on the Power Bar, and double-click QNIFEN.BK! to open a second copy of the file. (Opening two copies of the same document lets you view different parts at the same time.) WordPerfect tells you that the second copy will be read-only and that you will not be able to modify it without changing its name. Click Yes to open the copy.

7. Verify that you have two copies of the same document open by clicking *Window* on the menu bar. At the bottom of the menu, a second version of QNIFEN.BK! is listed.

8. Choose Cascade from the open Window menu. WordPerfect arranges the document windows like this:

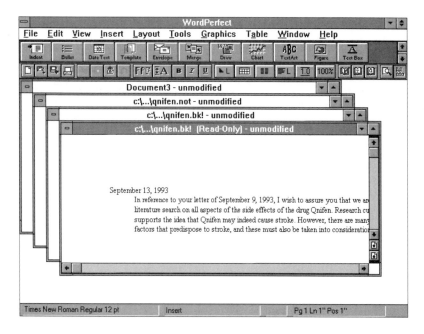

These simple techniques work equally well no matter how many documents you have open. (You can have nine documents open at one time, but three or four is the practical limit.)

Closing Documents

When you've finished working with a document, it's wise to close it to conserve your computer's memory. In this section, we'll show you three ways to close documents.

1. With the second copy of QNIFEN.BK! still active, click the small dash in the box at the left end of its title bar to display the Document Control menu, and then choose Close. Word-Perfect closes the document.

2. With QNIFEN.BK! active, choose the Close command from the File menu. (If you have made changes to this document, WordPerfect asks whether to save the document. Click No.)

3. Finally, choose Document3 from the Window menu, and then press Ctrl+F4, the Close command's shortcut key combination. (Again, click No if you're asked about saving changes.)

The current version of the memo (QNIFEN.NOT) is now the only document open on your screen.

Getting Help

Title bar descriptions

With WordPerfect for Windows, help is never far away. If you get stuck, you have several options, depending on what level of information you need. At the "memory jogger" end of the spectrum are the document window's title bar, which offers brief explanations of the highlighted command or the button to which you are pointing, and the status bar, which gives on-the-spot information about the status of some features. At the other end of the spectrum is the comprehensive reference manual. In between is WordPerfect's Help feature, which we'll briefly look at here.

The Help Feature

You can access the WordPerfect for Windows Help feature by choosing commands from the Help menu at the right end of the menu bar. The type of information displayed depends on which command you choose and what you are doing in WordPerfect at the time. The best way to explore the Help feature is to have WordPerfect itself show you around. Here's how to ask for a guided tour:

1. Choose the Contents command from the Help menu to display the Help window, and then click the window's Maximize button so that the window fills the entire screen, like this:

Coaches

To get step-by-step instructions on how to perform certain tasks in WordPerfect, you can enlist the help of a coach or two. Just choose Coach from the Help menu, and when the Coach dialog box appears, select a lesson from the list of those available, and click OK. The coach then guides you through the lesson steps. (And this coach won't make you sit on the sidelines if you make a mistake.)

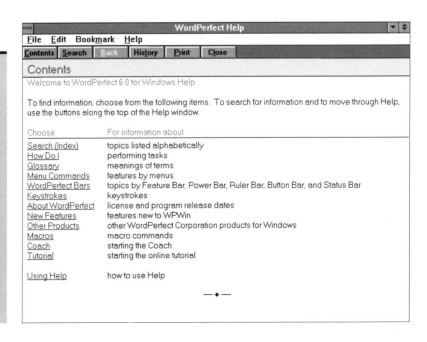

2. Click Using Help at the bottom of the window to display ◄─── information about the Help feature.

Getting help with Help

3. Read the information in the window, and then click the words with dotted underlines to display pop-up windows with information about the buttons on the Help window's Button Bar.

4. Click the Back button on the Help window's Button Bar to return to the Contents window, and take a moment to investigate other Help topics.

5. When you are ready, click the Close button to return to the document window.

Context-Sensitive Help

WordPerfect can give you *context-sensitive help* by displaying a Help window containing information about a particular command or dialog box. For example, suppose you want information about the Preferences command. You simply click the File menu, use the Down Arrow key to move the highlight to the Preferences command, and then press the F1 key to display a Help window with information about the command. If you have already chosen the Preferences command and want to find out more before you proceed, you can click the Help button in the Preferences dialog box to display the same information. (All dialog boxes have a Help button, so help with an option is never more than a mouse click away.)

Quitting WordPerfect for Windows

Well, that's it for the basic tour. We'll finish up by showing you how to end a WordPerfect for Windows session:

1. Choose Exit from the File menu.

2. If WordPerfect asks whether you want to save the changes you have made to the open document, click Yes.

Efficient Memos

What you will learn

Use WordPerfect's templates to quickly create professional-looking documents

Memorandum

To:	Dr. George Winters
CC:	Dr. Paul Reynolds
From:	Dr. Kaye Fox
Date:	September 16, 1993
Subject:	Case #312

Correct your text with simple editing techniques

The woman who is the complainant in Case #312 was seen by Dr. Reynolds on September 8. At that time he noted that she had been a heavy smoker for over 30 years. This is a new development, which I think we should investigate thoroughly.

Attached is an article from the New World Journal of Medicine on the association of cigarette smoking and the incidence of stroke in patients using the drug Qnifen. This is an up-to-date study from the University of Reedsport School of Medicine. Research currently supports the idea that Qnifen may indeed cause stroke. However, there are many health factors that predispose to stroke, and these must also be taken into consideration. Please review the article and give me your reaction as soon as possible.

Incorporate text from other documents

Copy or move words, sentences, or paragraphs with a few mouse clicks

With the advent of word processors, memos are easier to create than ever before. No more scribbled or laboriously typed notes. You can now turn out—in no time at all—neat, error-free memos recording who said what to whom, calling a meeting, or announcing a new policy. In the next few pages, we show you how to write, edit, and print a memo based on one of WordPerfect for Windows' memo templates. This template provides a basic memo structure (title, headings, and message area) that you can use again and again, plugging in new information each time.

WordPerfect provides several template files as starting points for the documents you create. In addition to the memo templates, you'll also find templates for letters, faxes, newsletters, and other standard documents. The template files all have descriptive names, so it's easy to locate the type of template you're looking for. In Chapter 4, we'll show you how to create your own templates and add them to WordPerfect's template "library."

The memo template we'll use is a plain, businesslike memo, but there is no reason why you shouldn't add a personal touch or two. After reading the other chapters in this book, you'll be able to dress up the memo template with borders or graphics, but for now, we'll keep things simple. Just remember that with WordPerfect, you can customize templates to meet your needs.

Using WordPerfect's Templates

Before you open the memo template, be sure your screen is clear. If you're at the DOS prompt, type *win* to load Windows, and then double-click the WPWin 6.0 icon to start WordPerfect for Windows. If a document is displayed on your screen, choose Close from the File menu. (If you've made any changes since the last time you saved the document, WordPerfect asks whether you want to save those changes; click Yes or No as appropriate.) That's it. Now for the memo:

1. If you're following along from Chapter 1, click the Template button you added to the Button Bar. Otherwise, choose Template from the File menu to display this dialog box:

As the Description box explains, every document is based on a template, and by default, all new documents are based on the STANDARD template.

The STANDARD template

2. Press the Up Arrow key to highlight different templates in the Document Template To Use list, and note the descriptions of each template as you go. As you can see, a wide variety of documents are available.

3. When MEMO3 is highlighted, click OK to open it.

4. When WordPerfect tells you that you can personalize the template, click OK. Then click Cancel to close the next dialog box. (If you want, you can complete this dialog box later on your own.) WordPerfect displays this document:

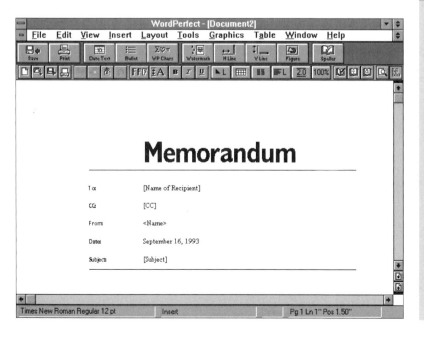

The correct date, every time

When you load WordPerfect's MEMO3 template, the Date line is already filled in with the correct date. Why? Because this line of the template contains a Date code. When WordPerfect encounters a Date code, it replaces the code with the current date recorded by your computer's clock/calendar. You can insert Date codes in a document by positioning the insertion point where you want the date to appear and choosing Date and then Date Code from the Insert menu.

As you can see, a different Button Bar now spans your screen. WordPerfect has provided a Button Bar containing the features it thinks you are likely to use when writing a memo.

5. The first thing to do is assign the memo a name. Click the Save button on the Power Bar (or the Button Bar). Because you have not yet given this file a name, WordPerfect displays the Save As dialog box, just as if you had chosen Save As from the File menu (see page 15).

6. Type *case312.mem* (for *Case #312 memo*), and press Enter.

7. Now type the memo's message. Press Ctrl+End and, using the magnified graphic below as a guide, type the first paragraph, press Enter twice to end the paragraph and create a blank line, type the second paragraph, and press Enter again:

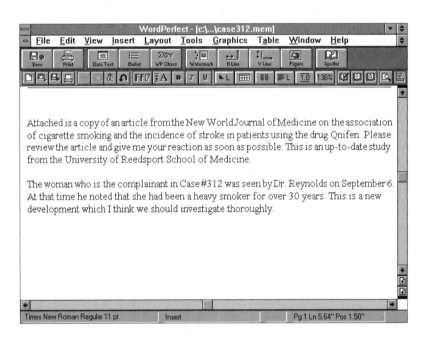

Turning off the Button Bar

The sample memo is short enough to fit easily on the screen, but when you type longer documents, you might want to turn off the Button Bar so that you can see more of your text in the window at the same time. Simply right-click the Button Bar, and then choose Hide Button Bar from the bottom of the QuickMenu. You can choose Button Bar from the View menu to turn on the Button Bar again.

8. Click the Save button on the Power Bar (or the Button Bar) to save your work.

Editing Basics

To fill in the memo's headings, you need to know some basic editing techniques. We'll start with the simplest methods and then move on to more advanced methods that will allow you to correct and revise your documents quickly and efficiently.

Deleting Text

You are probably already familiar with the Backspace key
(←), which deletes the character to the left of the insertion
point. To delete the character to the right of the insertion
point, you use the Delete key, which is located on the right side of
your keyboard (some keyboards have a key labeled *Del*). You
can delete more than one character at a time by selecting the
text you want to delete and then pressing the Delete key.

If you accidentally delete the wrong item, don't panic.
WordPerfect's Undo command was designed to avoid such
catastrophes. Simply click the Undo button on the Power Bar
or choose the Undo command from the Edit menu or press
Ctrl+Z to undo your last action. (Bear in mind that some
actions, such as saving a file, cannot be undone.)

Let's delete the existing text in the memo's headings and
insert our own information:

Filling in the memo's headings

1. Move the insertion point in front of the left square bracket in
   [Name of Recipient], press Shift+End to select to the end of
   the line, press Delete, and type *Dr. George Winters*.

2. Move the insertion point in front of the left square bracket in
   [CC], and press Ctrl+Backspace to delete the "word" *[CC]*.
   Then type *Dr. Paul Reynolds*.

3. Next, select the word *<Name>*, and type *Dr. Kaye Fox*. The
   selected text is deleted automatically when you begin typing.

4. Click an insertion point in front of the *S* in *September*, press
   Shift+End, and then press Backspace to delete the selection.
   Oops. That's not what you meant to do!

Undoing mistakes

5. To undelete the line, click the Undo button on the Power Bar.
   Whew! Remember, Undo can be used to undo only your most
   recent action; you must click the Undo button or choose the
   Undo command from the Edit menu immediately after you've
   made a mistake.

6. To complete the memo headings, replace *[Subject]* with *Case
   #312*. The results are shown on the next page.

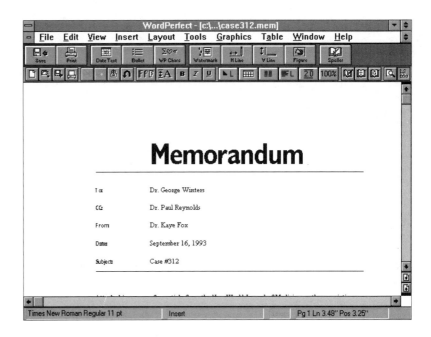

Undeleting Text

In addition to the invaluable Undo, WordPerfect provides an Undelete command, which allows you to restore any or all of your previous three deletions at the insertion point. To see how Undelete works, first make these deletions:

1. Click an insertion point in front of the *w* in *woman* in the second paragraph, hold down Shift, and click an insertion point in front of the *c* in *complainant* to select the text between the two clicks. Release the Shift key, and then press Delete.

2. Use the same technique to delete *a copy of* at the beginning of the first paragraph.

Now suppose you have second thoughts about deleting *woman who is the*. To undelete it, follow these steps:

1. Click an insertion point in front of the *c* in *complainant*, and choose Undelete from the Edit menu to display the Undelete dialog box:

Notice that WordPerfect has restored your most recent deletion (*a copy of*) at the insertion point.

2. Click the Previous button in the Undelete dialog box. The
words *woman who is the* appear at the insertion point.

3. Click the Restore button to undelete this deletion.

Overtyping Errors

Another way to correct minor errors is to use WordPerfect's
Typeover mode to overtype mistakes. Let's make a simple
correction using Typeover:

1. Move the insertion point in front of the *6* in *September 6*, and
press the Insert (Ins) key to turn on Typeover mode. The word
Typeover replaces *Insert* in the status bar at the bottom of
your screen.

Typeover mode

2. Type *8*. WordPerfect replaces the character to the right of the
insertion point with the character you typed.

3. Press the Insert key again to turn off Typeover mode and turn
on Insert mode.

Insert mode

4. Click an insertion point after the word *development* in the
second paragraph, and type a comma. WordPerfect inserts the
comma, pushing the text after the insertion point to the right
to make room.

5. Click the Save button to save your changes. From now on,
we won't tell you when to save the memo; just remember to
save frequently to safeguard your work.

Moving Text

When it comes to rearranging text, the Cut and Paste buttons
on WordPerfect's Power Bar are really handy. They let you
move blocks of text using just a few mouse clicks. Let's give
it a try:

1. Click an insertion point anywhere in the last sentence of the
first paragraph of the memo, and choose Select and then
Sentence from the Edit menu. WordPerfect selects the entire
sentence.

The QuickMenu for selected text

You can move, copy, and delete
selected text by right-clicking the
text and choosing the corresponding commands from the Quick-
Menu. In addition, you can use
the QuickMenu to apply common
formatting to the selected text.
(See Chapter 3 for more information about formatting.)

2. Click the Cut button on the Power Bar. WordPerfect deletes the highlighted sentence and moves it to a temporary storage place in your computer's memory called the *Clipboard*.

3. Click an insertion point in front of the *P* in *Please review*, and click the Paste button on the Power Bar. The sentence reappears in its new location.

4. Press the Spacebar to insert a space after the repositioned sentence.

If you accidentally cut the wrong text, you can restore the text to its original location by choosing Undo *before* you reposition the insertion point and click Paste.

Using the Cut and Paste buttons to move text is easy enough, but WordPerfect offers an even faster way: Drag And Drop Text. This technique is convenient because only the mouse is involved—you don't have to bother with buttons, menus, or the keyboard. Using Drag And Drop Text, let's transpose the two paragraphs of the memo:

Moving with Drag And Drop Text

1. If necessary, use the scroll bar to adjust the screen so that you can see both of the memo's paragraphs. Click an insertion point in the second paragraph, and choose Select and then Paragraph from the Edit menu.

2. Position the mouse pointer anywhere in the selected paragraph. Then hold down the left mouse button, and drag the

The Clipboard

The Windows Clipboard is a temporary storage space in your computer's memory. It is used to hold cut or copied information from all Windows applications. You can use it to transfer information from one place to another in a document, from one document to another, and from one application to another. The Clipboard can hold only one item of information at a time; cutting or copying a subsequent item overwrites the original Clipboard contents, so be sure to paste an item you need before performing another cut or copy operation. (Information erased with the Delete key is not stored on the Clipboard, so you can delete information using this key without disturbing the Clipboard's contents.) You can append a copy of a text or graphics selection to the existing contents of the Clipboard by using the Append command. Simply select the text or graphic you want to append, and then choose Append from the Edit menu. Because the Windows Clipboard is a temporary storage space, exiting Windows erases any information that is stored there, unless you save the Clipboard's contents in a file. You can save the file by switching to Program Manager, displaying the Clipboard window, and choosing Save As from the File menu. You can then load the file back onto the Clipboard when you restart Windows.

pointer—which now has two small boxes at its base—to just before the *A* in *Attached* at the beginning of the first paragraph. When you release the mouse button, this is the result:

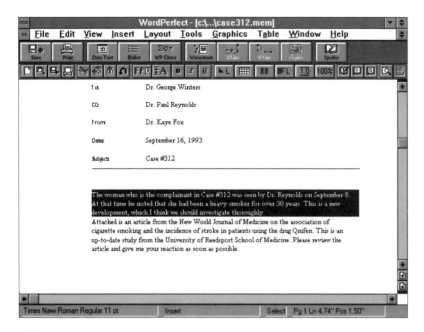

3. Click an insertion point before the *A* in *Attached*, and press Enter to insert a blank line between the two paragraphs.

You might think using Drag And Drop Text is a little awkward at first, but once you get the hang of it, you'll find it indispensable. So practice on your own, and before you know it, you'll be draggin' and droppin' every chance you get.

Copying Text

Now let's use a similar technique to copy a block of text in the memo:

1. With the insertion point still in the second paragraph of the memo, choose Select and then Paragraph from the Edit menu.

2. Click the Copy button on the Power Bar.

3. Press End, and then press the Down Arrow key to move the insertion point to a blank line below the memo.

4. Click the Paste button. WordPerfect inserts a copy of the paragraph, as shown at the top of the next page.

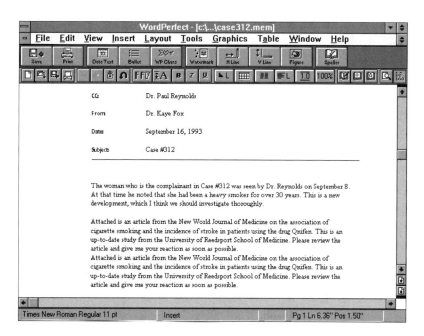

5. Now delete the second copy of the paragraph by selecting the paragraph and pressing Delete.

Copying with Drag And Drop Text

You can use Drag And Drop Text to copy text as well as to move it. Simply select the text you want to copy, drag the copy to its new location, and hold down the Ctrl key before you release the mouse button.

Copying Text from Another Document

One of the real advantages of a word processor is that it enables you to use the same text in several different documents. You type the text once and then use the simple techniques just described to transfer copies of the text elsewhere. Let's copy part of the note you wrote in Chapter 1 and paste it into CASE312.MEM:

More about Viewer

Right-clicking the Viewer window displays a QuickMenu of Viewer options that allow you to do such things as see the format of the file you are viewing, see the file's document summary (see page 77), wrap the file's text to fit the Viewer window, search for words and phrases, and copy text selected in the Viewer window to the Clipboard.

1. Click the Open button on the Power Bar or choose Open from the File menu.

2. In the Open File dialog box, click QNIFEN.NOT to highlight it, and then click the View button. WordPerfect opens a Viewer window in which it displays the contents of the selected file:

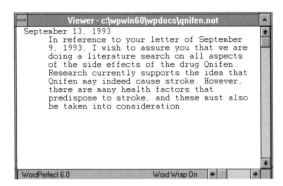

3. After verifying that this is the file you want, click OK. WordPerfect opens the note in its own document window.

4. In the note, click an insertion point in front of the *R* in *Research*, and then press Shift+Ctrl+End to select the last two sentences of the note.

5. Click the Copy button on the Power Bar to copy the two sentences, and choose Close from the File menu to close QNIFEN.NOT. (If WordPerfect asks whether you want to save changes to the note, click No.)

6. With the memo's window active, click an insertion point in front of the *P* in *Please review* in the second paragraph, click the Paste button, and then press the Spacebar to insert a space. The two sentences from the note are now incorporated in the memo, as shown on the following page.

QuickFinder

The WordPerfect for Windows QuickFinder feature is designed to help you quickly locate documents based on their filenames or extensions, their document summaries, or their actual contents. This powerful feature is particularly useful for businesses such as law firms or research organizations that sometimes need to extract related materials from huge numbers of files. You can choose QuickFinder from the File menu or click the QuickFinder command button in a dialog box to display the QuickFinder dialog box. You can then give WordPerfect a filename or filename pattern to search for (for example, entering *.LET* tells WordPerfect to search for all files with the LET extension). Alternatively, you can enter a word or phrase and then specify where WordPerfect is to conduct its search. Possible search limits include files in specific directories, certain parts of a document (for example, document summaries), and files with dates falling in a particular range. The fastest way to search the actual contents of your documents is to use the QuickFinder Indexer to create indexes of all the significant words in the documents so that WordPerfect can search the indexes rather than the files themselves.

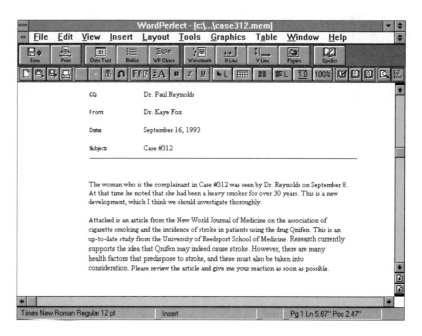

If you look very carefully, you will notice that the characters of the two inserted sentences are slightly larger than those of the surrounding memo text. Before you can correct this problem, you need to know more about fonts and formatting codes, which we cover in Chapter 3. In spite of this imperfection, let's move on now and see how to print the memo.

Printing Documents

When you installed WordPerfect for Windows, the installation program copied to your hard drive all the files necessary for WordPerfect and your printer to communicate. The printer we will use throughout this book is a Hewlett-Packard LaserJet 4M. If you are using a different printer, you might have a different choice of fonts. (We cover fonts in more detail on page 57.) Otherwise, you should have no difficulty printing the documents you create as you read this book.

Viewing the Memo

Although Page view shows your document as it will look when printed, you can see only as much of the document as will fit on one screen at a time. Before you actually print a document, you might want to see how it will look on the printed page. To view your document a full page at a time, you use WordPerfect's Zoom feature. Try the following:

Selecting a printer

When WordPerfect for Windows was installed on your computer, the installation program detected which printer was available and configured the program for that printer. If you have more than one printer available, you can switch from one to another by choosing the Select Printer command from the File menu. In the Select Printer dialog box, click the printer you want to use, and then click the Select button.

1. Press Ctrl+Home to move to the top of the memo, and then click the Page Zoom button on the Power Bar to display the memo like this:

Viewing an entire page

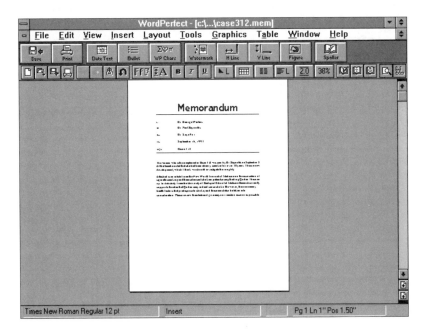

2. Press the Right Arrow key to move the blinking insertion point across the word *Memorandum*, and then press Home to move back to the beginning of the line. As you can see, navigating in a zoomed document is just like navigating in a document displayed at the default 100 percent size. You can also edit a zoomed document, though editing is not very practical at this percentage of reduction.

Magnifying documents

3. Point to the Zoom button on the Power Bar, hold down the left mouse button to display a pop-up list of display options, and select 200% to magnify your document.

4. Now try selecting a few of the other zoom options to see their effects, and then return the setting to 100%.

For documents that are more than one page long, you can view facing pages to ensure a pleasing presentation. Here's how:

1. First simulate a two-page document by clicking an insertion point in front of the *A* in *Attached* at the beginning of the second paragraph and pressing Ctrl+Enter to insert a page break at the insertion point.

Inserting page breaks

Two Page view

2. Choose Two Page from the View menu, and then press PgUp to display the memo like this:

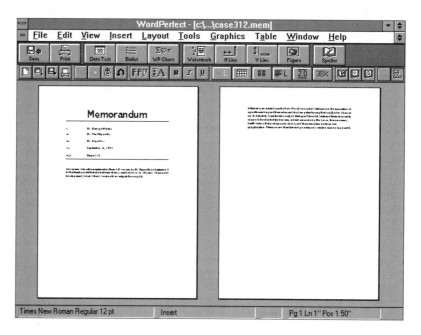

3. Point to the blank area below the text on the first page, click an insertion point at the end of the page, and press Delete to delete the page break. The second paragraph of the memo moves to the first page of the document, and the second page is now gray, indicating that it no longer exists.

4. Choose Page from the View menu to return to the familiar Page view.

Faxing documents

If you have a fax modem, a fax driver, and a fax program that runs under Windows, you can fax documents from within Word-Perfect for Windows. First select your fax driver in the Select Printer dialog box. Then click the Print button on the Power Bar, and click the Print button in the Print dialog box. WordPerfect sends your document to your fax modem instead of to your printer.

WordPerfect's views

WordPerfect's default viewing mode is Page, which shows all the elements of a document including margins, headers, and footnotes as they will appear on the printed page. (You can change the default by choosing Preferences from the File menu, clicking Display, selecting the View/Zoom option, and changing the Default View and Default Zoom settings.) You can see Page mode at various levels of magnification by clicking the Page Zoom and Zoom buttons on the Power Bar. Two Page mode shows two full pages side by side. Draft mode shows text and graphics as they will appear when printed but does not calculate page breaks or show page elements, such as headers and page numbers.

Sending the File to the Printer

Now for the real test. Assuming that your printer is turned on and ready to go, follow along while we print the memo:

1. Click the Print button on the Power Bar (or the Button Bar) to display the Print dialog box:

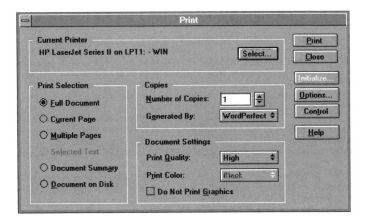

Take a moment to look over the options in the Print dialog box. You can control exactly how much of your document is printed by using the options in the Print Selection group box. You can also print a Document Summary (see page 77), and you can print a document directly from disk without loading it into WordPerfect. You can specify the number of copies to be printed, the print resolution, and whether to print graphics.

2. Be sure the Full Document option is selected in the Print Selection group box, and then click Print. WordPerfect sends the CASE312.MEM file to the printer, and printing begins.

If the printout of the memo doesn't look quite right, it's probably because your printer can't print some of the formatting used in the memo template. Otherwise, the printed memo should look like the one on page 25.

Now follow the step below so that you can begin Chapter 3 with a clean document window:

1. Choose Close from the File menu, and when WordPerfect asks whether you want to save your changes, click Yes to save CASE312.MEM and clear the screen.

Mailing documents

If your system is set up to send and receive electronic mail using a standard protocol, the Word-Perfect for Windows installation program detects your e-mail program. You can then mail a document from within WordPerfect by simply choosing the Mail command from the File menu, making the usual settings, and then sending the file on its way.

Business Letters

What you will learn

Fox & Associates

Medical Malpractice Consultants
1224 Evergreen Road, Lake Oswego, OR 97035

September 21, 1993

Mr. David Robertson
Sullivan, Duffy and Bridge, Attorneys at Law
145 Salmon Street
Portland, OR 97201

RE: CASE #312, REBECCA BRAND V. MIDVALLEY CLINIC

Dear Mr. Robertson:

Dr. George Winters and I have reviewed the medical files in the above case and have come to an opinion. We conclude that Rebecca Brand's stroke may have been exacerbated by her use of the drug Qnifen. However, in her case *other risk factors may have been equally or more important.*

A number of case reports have associated stroke with Qnifen administration over several years. Patients taking Qnifen are frequently also taking many other drugs; however, the association of stroke with these drugs in the absence of Qnifen has not been documented.

The other risk factors that may also have played a role in Rebecca Brand's stroke are the following:

    1. She is more than 59 years old.

    2. She has smoked cigarettes for over 30 years.

    3. She has mild hypertension.

Age, smoking, and hypertension are well-known risk factors for stroke.

I hope this summary of our opinion will be of help to you. Please call upon me for further information should you require it.

Sincerely,

Kaye E. Fox, Ph.D.

Whether you're writing letters for business or personal use, WordPerfect can simplify the entire process by making light work of tasks such as detecting and correcting spelling errors and adjusting margins. In this chapter, we build on what you learned in Chapter 2 and show you how to prepare a professional-looking letter.

The letter we use for the examples in this chapter is shown below. Start by typing this letter or one of your own. To follow along, you must include misspellings (such as *reviewe*, *Qnifan*, and *mald*), double words (such as *the the*), and mixed-up cases (such as *pLease*), and you should include a numbered list. Press the Enter key to add any necessary blank lines. Then save the letter as CASE312.LET.

Fox & Associates
Medical Malpractice Consultants
1224 Evergreen Road
Lake Oswego, OR 97035

September 21, 1993

Mr. David Robertson
Sullivan, Duffy and Bridge, Attorneys at Law
145 Salmon Street
Portland, OR 97201

Re: Case #312, Rebecca Brand v. Midvalley Clinic

Dear Mr. Robertson:

Dr. George Winters and I have reviewe the medical files in the above case and have come to an opinion. We conclude that Rebecca Brand's stroke may have been exacerbated by her use of the drug Qnifan. However, in her case other risk factors may have been equally or more important.

A number of case reports have associated stroke with Qnifan administration over several years. Patients taking Qnifan are frequently also taking many other drugs; however, the the association of stroke with these drugs in the absence of Qnifan has not been documented.

The other risk factors that may also have played a role in Rebecca Brand's stroke are the following:

1. She is more than 59 years old.
2. She has smoked cigarettes for over 30 years.
3. She has mald hypertension.
Age, smoking, and hypertension are well-known risk factors for stroke.

I hope this summary of our opinion will be of help to you. pLease call upon me for further information should you require it.

Sincerely,

Kaye E. Fox, Ph.D.

Fine-Tuning the Letter's Contents

Before you modify the way any document looks, you should be sure it accurately says what you want it to say. If you spend time formatting a letter so that it fits on one page and then make major content changes, such as adding a sentence or two, your formatting efforts may be wasted. In this section, the changes you'll make are small, but they are significant in terms of the impression your letter will make on its readers. We show you how to use the powerful Find and Replace commands and then how to put the Speller program through its paces. With these features at your fingertips, you'll be able to mop up errors and fix inconsistencies in no time.

Finding and Replacing Text

With the Find command, you can move quickly to any location in a document by giving WordPerfect a word, phrase, or code to find (called a *search string*). You use the Replace command to locate a specific word, phrase, or code and replace it with a new word, phrase, or code.

Search strings

Let's use the Find command in the CASE312.LET document to locate the word *Qnifan*:

1. Press Ctrl+Home to be sure the insertion point is at the beginning of the letter.

2. Choose the Find command from the Edit menu to display this Find Text dialog box:

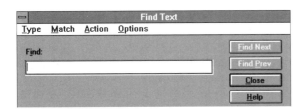

3. Type *Qnifan* in the Find edit box, and then click the Find Next button. WordPerfect instantly highlights the first occurrence of *Qnifan*.

4. Click the Find Next button to find the second occurrence of *Qnifan*.

Find options

The Find Text dialog box provides several menus with commands for customizing searches. For example, if you choose the Whole Word command from the Match menu and then enter *cat* as the search string, WordPerfect will not stop on *category* or *catalog*. To perform a case-sensitive search, choose Case from the Match menu; then if you enter *Cat*, WordPerfect finds only *Cat* and not *cat*. To extend the selection from the insertion point to the search string, choose Extend Selection from the Action menu. To position the insertion point before or after the matched search string, choose the appropriate command from the Action menu.

Searching backward

5. Click the Find Prev button to move back to the first occurrence of *Qnifan*.

6. Click the Close button to close the Find Text dialog box.

If you have been following along with previous examples, you know that the word *Qnifan* should actually be *Qnifen*. You can quickly correct this error by using the Replace command, as follows:

1. Press Ctrl+Home to move the insertion point to the beginning of the document.

Replacing text

2. Choose Replace from the Edit menu to display the Find And Replace Text dialog box:

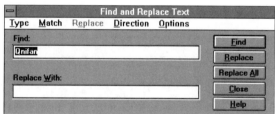

Notice that *Qnifan* still appears in the Find edit box, left over from our previous search, and that nothing appears in the Replace With edit box. (Replacing a search string with nothing can actually be a convenient way to delete certain words, phrases, or codes from your document.)

3. Click the Replace With edit box, and type *Qnifen*.

4. Click the Find button. WordPerfect highlights the first occurrence of the word *Qnifan*.

5. Click Replace. WordPerfect replaces the first *Qnifan* with *Qnifen* and moves to the second *Qnifan*.

6. Click Replace All. WordPerfect moves through the document, automatically replacing all the remaining occurrences of *Qnifan* with *Qnifen*.

7. When the replace operation is complete, click Close to close the dialog box and return to the document window.

8. Now with all four *Qnifens* in place, save the letter.

Finding or replacing codes

To find or replace codes, choose Codes from the Match menu of the Find Text or Find And Replace Text dialog box. When the Codes dialog box appears, highlight the code you want to find or replace, and then click Insert to enter the code in the Find edit box. The Codes dialog box remains open so that you can enter another code in the Replace With edit box (or you can close the dialog box and replace the code with nothing). Then click Find or Replace to find or replace the code. To narrow the search for a specific code, choose Specific Codes from the Type menu, select a code, and then select the appropriate options in the resulting Find Text or Find And Replace Text dialog box.

Checking Spelling

Nobody spells or types perfectly all the time. Fortunately, WordPerfect's Speller program detects not only spelling errors but also double words and inappropriate capitalization. What's more, Speller is so easy to use that you'll have no excuse for not spell-checking every WordPerfect document you create.

Speller works by comparing the words in your document with the words in its dictionary. If Speller can't find a matching word in its dictionary, it displays a list of alternative spellings. If the word is an error, you can correct it either by selecting a replacement word from Speller's Suggestions list box or by editing the word yourself. If the word is not an error— for example, Speller might stumble over obscure slang terms and some proper names, such as *Sullivan* and *Rebecca*—you can click the Skip Once button to tell Speller to ignore this instance of the word but stop for future instances, or you can click the Skip Always button to tell Speller not to stop for that word again.

Slang and proper names

With the letter displayed on your screen, follow these steps to check your spelling:

1. Move the insertion point to the beginning of the letter, and click the Speller button on the Power Bar. WordPerfect displays this dialog box:

Starting Speller

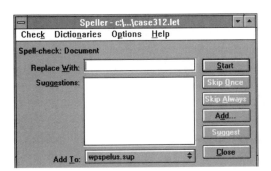

2. Click the Start button. Speller starts checking your document, stopping when it finds the first problem, as shown on the following page.

Spell-checking as you write

If you are unsure of the spelling of a word, simply highlight the word and click the Speller button. WordPerfect gives you instant feedback, enabling you to correct your work in progress.

3. Speller has stopped on the name *Sullivan*. Click the Skip Always button to tell Speller to ignore this and any other instances of that name in the document. Do the same when Speller stops on *Rebecca* and *Midvalley*.

4. Speller stops on *reviewe*, displaying this list of possible replacements:

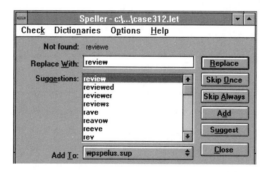

5. Select *reviewed* in the Suggestions list box, and then click the Replace button.

6. When Speller stops on *Qnifen*, click Skip Always.

7. When Speller stops on the double words *the the*, click Replace to delete the second *the*.

8. When Speller stops on *mald*, double-click the suggested word *mad* in the Replace With edit box to select it, type *mild*, and click Replace.

9. When Speller stops on *pLease*, select *Please* in the Suggestions list box, and then click Replace to correct the capitalization error.

Supplementary dictionaries

WordPerfect attaches a supplementary dictionary to every document you create. If you want Speller to ignore certain words when it spell-checks your document, you can add these words to the supplementary dictionary. To work with this dictionary or to create and edit your own supplementary dictionaries, choose Supplementary from Speller's Dictionaries menu, and then add, edit, or delete words as necessary.

10. For the proper name *Kaye* and the abbreviation *Ph.D.*, click the Skip Once button.

11. Speller displays a message box when the spell-check is complete. Click Yes to return to the document window, and then save your corrected letter.

Take the time to experiment with Speller. The program is not infallible, but running it on important documents might save you from unpleasant typographical embarrassments.

Fine-Tuning the Letter's Appearance

The letter you've typed is fairly presentable, but you can do a lot to fine-tune its appearance. In this section, we show you how to format documents by applying attributes and changing the justification, line spacing, indentation, fonts, and margins.

Applying Attributes

You apply *attributes* to your text to dress it up and to emphasize certain words. WordPerfect allows you to apply the most common attributes—bold, italic, and underlining—with just the click of a button. Try this:

1. Select the letter's subject line (the line that starts with *Re:*), and click the Bold button on the Power Bar.

Bold
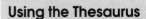

2. Select the words *other risk factors may have been equally or more important* at the end of the first paragraph, and click the Italic button on the Power Bar.

Italic

Checking grammar

To catch errors of grammar, syntax, and improper word usage in your documents, use WordPerfect's grammar-checker, Grammatik. This program applies common grammar rules to your text to identify potential problems, suggest corrections where appropriate, and provide helpful explanations if you request them. During a grammar-check, WordPerfect also spell-checks the document and accumulates statistics that assess the document's readability. To run Grammatik, press Ctrl+Home to move to the top of the document, and then click the Grammatik button on the Power Bar. You can ignore "problems" you don't want to correct; implement suggested replacements; and make changes directly to your document without quitting Grammatik. When Grammatik finishes checking the document, you can save your changes to a custom writing style and view readability statistics.

Using the Thesaurus

WordPerfect's Thesaurus is a very handy way to find alternate words for your documents. Simply select the word you want to change, and click the Thesaurus button on the Power Bar. WordPerfect then displays a list of synonyms and antonyms for the selected word.

Underline

3. Select the line that begins with the word *Age* below the numbered list, and click the Underline button on the Power Bar. Here are the results:

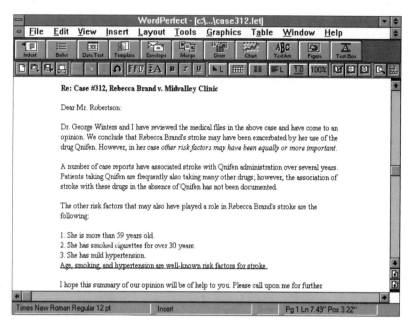

What else can we do to dress up the letter? Let's add weight to the subject line by making it uppercase. Here's how:

1. Select the entire subject line, and choose Convert Case and then Uppercase from the Edit menu.

2. Click anywhere in the document to remove the selection so that you can see this result:

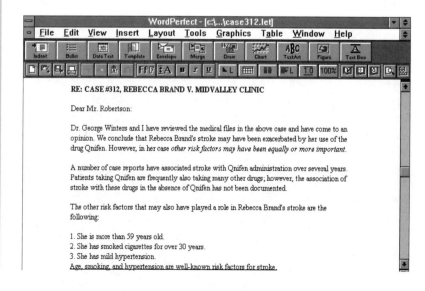

Other attributes

In addition to using Power Bar buttons to make the selected text bold, italic, or underlined, you can apply other appearance attributes, such as Redline, Strikeout, and Hidden, by choosing Font from the Layout menu. Redline is often used to identify information that has been added to a document, and Strikeout can be used to identify suggested deletions. (These attributes are also used by the Compare Document feature to designate differences between one version of a document and another.) The Hidden attribute is often used for questions and comments that you want to be visible when a document is displayed on the screen but invisible when the document is printed. (You can also use the Comment feature to embed comments in a document; see the tip on page 107.)

3. Once again, click the Save button to save the letter.

Justifying and Aligning Text

The way you justify and align your text affects the way it looks and can determine its impact. Generally, you align a single line of text, and you justify multiple lines.

The word *justification* means to arrange lines of text in such a way that all the lines come out even at one or both of the margins. WordPerfect offers five justification types: Left, Center, Right, Full, and All.

This is an example of left justification. These lines are even at the left margin and uneven (ragged) at the right margin. Justify letters this way when you want them to appear informal and friendly.

Left justification

This is an example of center justification. These lines are centered between the left and right margins. Center justification is great for setting off multiple lines of text.

Center justification

This is an example of right justification. These lines are even at the right margin and uneven at the left margin. This type of justification is rarely used in letters.

Right justification

This is an example of full justification. The lines are even at both the right and left margins. Justify letters this way when you want them to appear formal and professional.

Full justification

This is an example of all justification. The lines have been stretched to reach the left and right margins by adding space between the letters and words. This format is useful for banner headings.

All justification

When you start WordPerfect, left justification is the default, meaning that if you print the letter now, the lines will be uneven at the right margin. If you want a different type of justification, you can change the setting before or after you type the document. Follow these steps to switch to full justification:

1. To change the justification for an entire document, the insertion point must be at the very beginning of the document, so press Ctrl+Home.

2. Point to the Justification button on the Power Bar (where the letter *L* appears), hold down the left mouse button to display a pop-up list of options, and select Full. The letter *F* now appears on the Justification button.

3. Scroll down to see how the letter looks with its new format, noticing that the lines are now even at both the left and right margins:

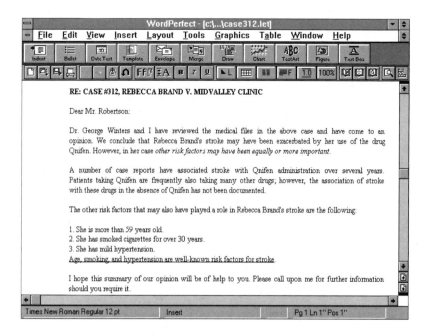

Now let's right-align the letter's date:

1. Click an insertion point in front of the date, display the Justification button's pop-up list, and select Right. Oops! All the text from the insertion point on has moved to the right.

2. Click the Undo button to restore full justification so that we can try a different method.

Right alignment

3. With the insertion point still in front of the date, choose Line and then Flush Right from the Layout menu. This time, only the date moves to the right:

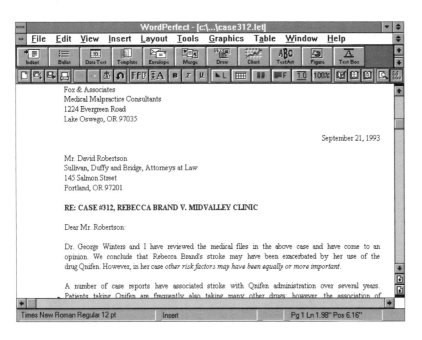

Now let's center the lines of the return address. Try these two methods:

1. Press Ctrl+Home to move to the top of the letter, and choose Line and then Center from the Layout menu. The first line is now centered.

2. Instead of center-aligning each of the remaining three lines individually, select the lines and then select Center from the Justification button's pop-up list. All three lines are centered at once:

Center alignment

Realigning partial lines

You can choose Line and then Center or Flush Right from the Layout menu to center or right-align part of a line of text. For example, if you type *Left*, choose Line and then Center, type *Center*, choose Line and then Flush Right, and type *Right*, the result looks like this:

Left   Center   Right

To see an example of all-justified text, complete this step:

1. Select the entire subject line, and then select All from the Justification button's pop-up list. The line now stretches from the left to right margins.

Taking a Look at WordPerfect's Codes

When you apply attributes, such as bold or italic, or change a document's justification or alignment, WordPerfect inserts codes in your document. These codes determine the way your document looks both on the screen and when printed. You cannot see the codes in the normal document window, but you can see them in WordPerfect's Reveal Codes area. By displaying this area, you can check the position of your formatting codes to be sure your document will appear on the printed page exactly the way you want it to.

To display the Reveal Codes area, follow these steps:

Displaying the Reveal Codes area → 1. Press Ctrl+Home to move to the top of the letter, and choose Reveal Codes from the View menu. The screen splits in two, with the letter displayed in both parts, as shown here:

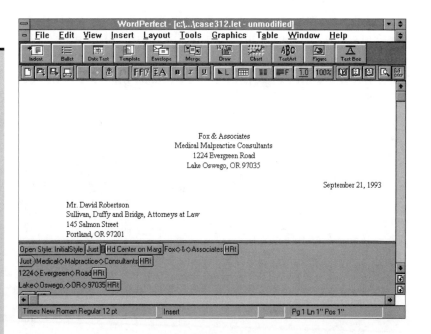

Manipulating the Reveal Codes area

You can increase the size of the Reveal Codes area by pointing to the top border of the area, holding down the mouse button, and dragging upward. Decrease the size by dragging downward. To quickly display the Reveal Codes area and adjust its size at the same time, point to the black bar above the up arrow on the vertical scroll bar, and drag downward, releasing the mouse button when the area is the size you want. Hide the area by dragging its top border downward off the screen.

The normal document window occupies the top two-thirds of the screen, and the Reveal Codes area occupies the bottom one-third. You can move the insertion point, which is a solid block, around the Reveal Codes area just as you would move it around the document window.

The first code is Open Style: InitialStyle, which WordPerfect automatically inserts at the beginning of your documents. This code contains the information WordPerfect uses to control the general appearance of your documents. (We discuss initial codes in more detail on page 64.) The next code— Just—was added by WordPerfect when you changed the justification of the entire document to Full (see page 50).

2. Click the first Just code. It expands to Just: Full so that you can see the type of justification that is controlling the appearance of your document at that point. Full justification is in fact overridden by the next code—Hd Center on Marg, which means *force this line (Hd) to center between the left and right margins (Marg).* WordPerfect inserted this alignment code when you chose Line and Center from the Layout menu (see page 51).

Expanding codes

3. Click the second Just code, which expands to Just: Center. This is where you changed the justification of the second, third, and fourth lines of the return address to center justification (see page 51). Because you selected these lines, WordPerfect applied the justification change only to them by inserting a Just: Center code at the beginning of the selection to turn on center justification and a Just: Full code at the end to restore the full justification that you specified earlier for the entire document.

4. Examine the remaining codes in the Reveal Codes area by pressing the Down Arrow key. Notice particularly the "paired codes," such as Bold and Italic. These codes have on and off components that tell WordPerfect when to turn the attribute on and when to turn it off.

Notice also the hard return (HRt) codes scattered throughout the letter. WordPerfect inserts these codes every time you press Enter. You'll also see soft return (SRt) codes, which indicate line breaks inserted by WordPerfect. They are called

Deleting formatting in the Reveal Codes area

Often the quickest way of turning off attributes and removing other types of formatting is to delete their codes in the Reveal Codes area. Simply move the insertion point before or after the code, and press Delete or Backspace to remove it. If the code is one of a pair, WordPerfect automatically removes the other code.

soft returns because their position changes as you edit the document.

5. Choose Reveal Codes from the View menu to close the Reveal Codes area.

Don't be intimidated by all the coding. If you're like most people, when you get used to the codes, you will think nothing of working in both the document window and the Reveal Codes area. You might even find editing and formatting documents in the Reveal Codes area just as easy as in the document window.

Adjusting Line Spacing

Usually, regular paragraphs in a letter are single-spaced, but sometimes you will want to change the spacing for specific elements, or you might want to specify double-spacing or even triple-spacing for drafts. WordPerfect's default line-spacing setting is 1—single-spacing. Changing this setting to 2 produces double-spacing, and changing it to 3 produces triple-spacing. You can enter numbers like 1.5 or 2.4 for more precise control. Follow these steps to double-space the numbered list in the letter:

Double-spacing

1. Use the vertical scroll bar to scroll the numbered list into view, click an insertion point in front of the number 1, and choose Line and then Spacing from the Layout menu to display this dialog box:

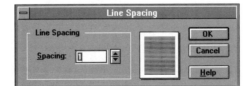

2. In the Spacing edit box, type *2* for double-spacing, and press Enter. (You can also click the arrows to the right of the edit box to adjust this setting up or down.) Now all of the text from the numbered list to the bottom of the letter is double-spaced, as shown here:

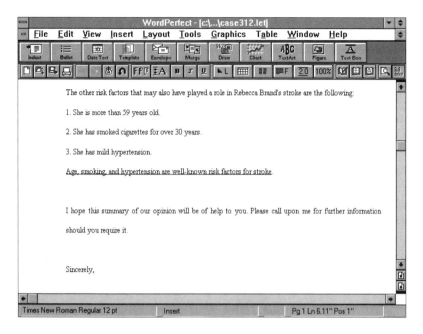

It's important to remember that when you add formatting to a document, you're also adding codes. The formatting remains in effect from the point in the document where a code turns it on to the point where another code turns it off. Because you want only the numbered list to be double-spaced, you must insert a code for single-spacing after the numbered list, as follows:

1. Move the insertion point to the *A* in *Age* (the first word following the numbered list), and choose Line and then Spacing from the Layout menu.

2. In the Spacing edit box, type *1* for single-spacing, and press Enter. The lines following the numbered list are now single-spaced.

3. Choose Reveal Codes from the View menu to see the line spacing codes that WordPerfect has inserted in the letter. Choose Reveal Codes again to close the Reveal Codes area.

Indenting Paragraphs

The formatting we've added to the letter has improved its looks, but it could still use a touch or two. For example, we can indent the numbered list to make it stand out.

Automatic code placement

WordPerfect automatically puts codes that control paragraph formatting, such as justification and line spacing, at the beginning of the paragraph in which the insertion point is located. In other words, you don't have to move the insertion point to the beginning of the paragraph before changing the format.

In WordPerfect, you can create several kinds of indents. You can indent whole paragraphs from just the left or from both the left and right; you can create hanging indents, where the second and subsequent lines of a paragraph are indented but the first line is not; and you can indent just the first line of a paragraph to more clearly separate it from the preceding one. How much you indent is a function of current tab settings. WordPerfect's default tab settings are at 1/2-inch intervals, but you can increase or decrease these intervals using the Tab Set command. (We talk more about this command on page 109.) For now, we'll show you three simple techniques for indenting the numbered list in CASE312.LET:

1. Click an insertion point in front of the 1 in the first line of the numbered list, and then click the Indent button on the Button Bar. WordPerfect indents the paragraph a half-inch.

2. Click an insertion point in front of the 2 in the second line of the list, and choose Paragraph and then Indent from the Layout menu.

3. Now try a keyboard shortcut. Click an insertion point in front of the 3 in the third line, and press the F7 key. Here are the results:

First line indents (and outdents)

You can indent the first line of each new paragraph by choosing Paragraph and then Format from the Layout menu and specifying the size of the indent as the First Line Indent setting. Specifying a negative First Line Indent setting, such as –0.5, creates a hanging indent, where the first line is outdented from the rest of the lines in the paragraph. (You can also create outdents by choosing Paragraph and then Back Tab from the Layout menu.)

WordPerfect - [c:\...\case312.let]

File   Edit   View   Insert   Layout   Tools   Graphics   Table   Window   Help

The other risk factors that may also have played a role in Rebecca Brand's stroke are the following:

    1. She is more than 59 years old.

    2. She has smoked cigarettes for over 30 years.

    3. She has mild hypertension.

Age, smoking, and hypertension are well-known risk factors for stroke.

I hope this summary of our opinion will be of help to you. Please call upon me for further information should you require it.

Sincerely,

Kaye E. Fox, Ph.D.

Times New Roman Regular 12 pt   Insert   Pg 1 Ln 6.90" Pos 1.50"

Changing the Font Face and Size

The appearance of your printed WordPerfect documents is a function of the fonts you use for your text. Which fonts you have available is determined by your printer. Most printers can print several fonts. WordPerfect 6 for Windows supports many fonts and provides internal font support so that you can view the fonts on your screen as they will appear when printed.

Fonts come in many shapes and sizes, but all fonts belong to one of two categories: *monospace* fonts (also known as *fixed pitch* fonts) and *proportional* fonts. Courier is an example of a monospace font. When you print a document in Courier, every character occupies the same amount of space. In other words, an *m* takes up the same amount of space as an *l*, as shown here:

Monospace versus proportional fonts

mmmmmmmmmmm
llllllllll

Times New Roman is an example of a proportional font, in which every character occupies an amount of space that is proportional to its width. So an *m* takes up much more space than an *l*, as shown here:

mmmmmmmmmm
llllllllll

The appearance of your documents is not only affected by the font you use but also by the font size. In general, fonts are measured in terms of their height—the distance from the bottom of *descenders* (the part of letters such as *p* that descend below the line) to the top of *ascenders* (the part of letters such as *h* that ascend above the line). The unit of measure is called a *point* (abbreviated *pt*), and 1 point equals 1/72 inch. Depending on the font, you will probably use sizes between 9 points and 13 points for ordinary text and larger sizes for titles and headings. (The text in this book is 12.5 points, and the headings are 16 points, 14 points, and 12 points.)

Font size

With older versions of most word processors, the default font was generally Courier 10 pt, which resembled the output of a typewriter. If you wanted a more professional look, you had to manually change the font and possibly its size. With WordPerfect 6 for Windows, the default font and size is Times New Roman 12 pt, which produces perfectly acceptable, businesslike results. However, you might want to change these defaults, either for an entire document or for selected elements. Try this:

Switching fonts

1. Press Ctrl+Home to move to the top of your document, and click the Font Face button on the Power Bar to display a drop-down list of the fonts available for your printer, with Times New Roman, the current font, selected.

2. Click Courier New to close the list and switch to that font.

Adjusting size

3. Now change the size by clicking the Font Size button on the Power Bar and selecting 10 from the drop-down list of sizes. Here are the results:

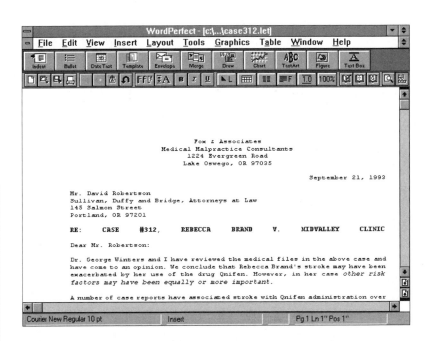

Notice that when you change the font or font size for a document, as we just did, WordPerfect automatically reformats the text in the document. If the letter's text now wraps differently than before, it's all part of the master plan.

4. The letter now looks pretty clunky. Use the Font Face and Font Size buttons to try a few other font and size combinations, and then return the letter to Times New Roman 12 pt.

Copying formatting

To quickly copy the formatting from one block of text to another, select the formatted text, and click the QuickFormat button on the Button Bar or choose QuickFormat from the Layout menu. Then simply drag the paint-roller pointer over the text you want to format. WordPerfect applies all the font and attribute formats of the selected text to the "painted" text. Click the QuickFormat button or choose the QuickFormat command again to stop "painting."

You've seen that changing the font and size while the insertion point is at the top of the document affects the appearance of the entire document. But you can also make changes to just part of the document. Follow these steps:

1. Select the first line of the return address, and choose the Font command from the Layout menu to display this dialog box:

Changing the font of a
selected element

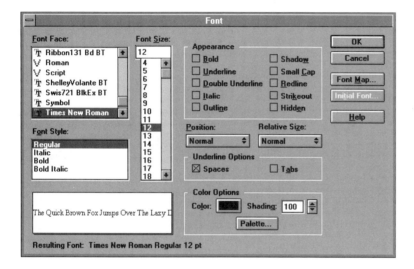

As you can see, the Font dialog box allows you to select a font and size, apply attributes, and change various other text characteristics all in one place. The box in the bottom-left corner shows sample text as it would appear with your selections implemented.

2. Select 24 in the Font Size box, and click the Bold check box in the Appearance group box. Then use the Up and Down Arrow keys to scroll through the Font Face list, checking the sample box to see what each font will look like.

3. When you have found a font that produces a strong look (we selected Swis721 BlkEx BT), click OK to return to the document window with your selections implemented.

4. Select the *F* in *Fox*, click the Font Size button on the Power Bar, and select 36. Repeat this step for the *A* in *Associates*.

5. Select the *Medical Malpractice Consultants* line, change the font size to 18 pt, and make the text italic. The return address now looks as shown on the next page.

Other font options

In the Font dialog box, you can superscript or subscript selected text by using the options on the Position pop-up list, and you can select from a number of predetermined sizes, such as Large and Small, by using the options on the Relative Size pop-up list. You can also specify whether the Underline and Double Underline attributes should apply to spaces and tabs, and you can change the color and shading of the selected text in the Color Options group box.

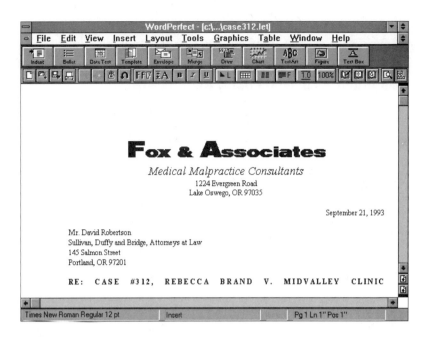

6. Save your work before moving on.

Adding Borders and Shading

With WordPerfect 6 for Windows, you can add borders and shading to paragraphs with a few clicks of the mouse button. In this section, we'll add a border and shading to the return address at the top of the letter to give it the look of a letterhead. In the next chapter, we'll show you how to create even fancier letterheads. Follow these steps:

1. Select the four lines of the return address, and choose Paragraph and then Border/Fill from the Layout menu to display this dialog box:

Visual border selection

To see the types of borders that result when you select border options from the Border Style drop-down list, you can click the box to the right of Border Style and then select from a palette of icons depicting the borders. If a border is almost, but not exactly, what you want, you can select it and then customize it by clicking the Customize Style button (see page 142 for more information).

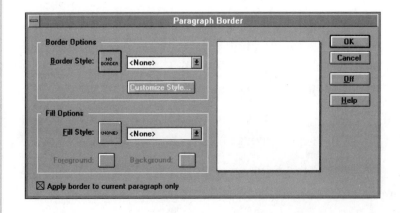

2. In the Border Options group box, click the down arrow at the right end of the Border Style option box, which currently contains *<None>*, and select Single from the drop-down list.

3. In the Fill Options group box, click the down arrow at the right end of the Fill Style options box, and select 20% Fill.

4. Click OK. WordPerfect draws a border stretching from margin to margin around all four selected paragraphs and fills the space within the border with a 20 percent gray shading. (This gray shade is created with an even distribution of 20 percent black dots and 80 percent white dots. A 30 percent gray shading would be darker because it would have 30 percent black dots and 70 percent white dots, and a 10 percent shading would be lighter because the distribution would be 10 percent black and 90 percent white.)

5. To put a little more space between the last line of the return address and the bottom border, click an insertion point after the *5* in the ZIP code, and press Enter. The border and shading grow to enclose the new blank line, and your screen now looks like this:

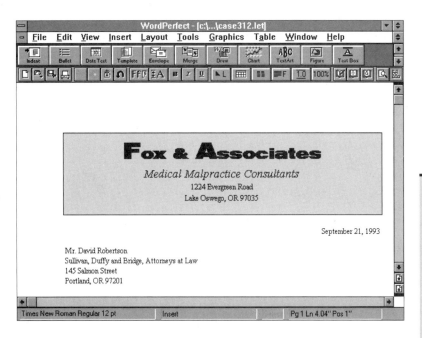

6. One more adjustment: The return address would look better if the address itself were on one line. It's easy to make this kind of edit in the Reveal Codes area, so choose Reveal Codes

Color shading

If you have a color printer or your documents are designed for screen presentation only, you might want to select a color for your fill patterns by clicking the icons to the right of the Foreground and Background options and then selecting colors from the palettes to produce exciting visual effects.

from the View menu, move the insertion point in front of the *L* in *Lake*, and press Backspace to delete the HRt code at the end of the preceding line. Now type a comma and a space, and choose the Reveal Codes command again to close the Reveal Codes area.

Setting Margins

One way to balance the proportions of a letter is to change its margins. WordPerfect's default left, right, top, and bottom margin settings are 1 inch. You might want to shorten a long letter by decreasing the left and right margins or lengthen a short letter by increasing those margins. You can also adjust the top and bottom margins to achieve the desired effect. Let's see what margin changes we can make to improve the positioning of the letter on the page:

Checking text position

1. Press Ctrl+Home to be sure the insertion point is at the beginning of the letter, and then click the Page Zoom button on the Power Bar to see the entire page:

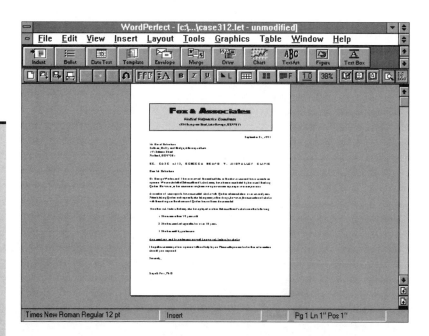

Displaying paragraph marks

As an alternative to working in the Reveal Codes area, you can display nonprinting characters such as paragraph marks, spaces, and tabs by choosing the Show ¶ command from the View menu. You can then delete characters such as paragraph marks without working "in the dark." Choose the command again to hide the characters.

The letter sits a little low on the page, so let's move it up by decreasing the top margin and then increase the left and right margins so that the letter continues to occupy the full length of the page.

2. Choose Margins from the Layout menu to display the Margins dialog box:

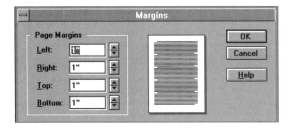

3. Change both the Left and Right settings to *1.25*, change the Top setting to *0.5*, and click OK to return to the letter.

Using the Margins command changes the margins for the entire document. What if you want to adjust the margins for only one paragraph? Try this:

1. Select the entire subject line below the recipient's address, and choose Paragraph and then Format from the Layout menu to display this dialog box:

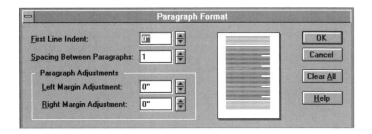

2. In the Paragraph Adjustments group box, click the upward-pointing arrowhead at the right end of the Left Margin Adjustment edit box until its setting is *0.700*.

3. Repeat step 2 for the Right Margin Adjustment setting, and click OK. Remove the highlight so that you can see the result, as shown on the next page.

Centering vertically

Letters, particularly short ones, look best when they are centered on the page—that is, placed approximately the same distance from the top of the page as from the bottom. You could achieve this effect by adjusting your top and bottom margins, but Word-Perfect provides an easier way: Choose Page and then Center from the Layout menu to display the Center Page(s) dialog box, select the Current Page option, and click OK. (If you want to center more than one page, you can select the Current And Subsequent Pages option instead; the insertion point must be located on the page where you want centering to begin.)

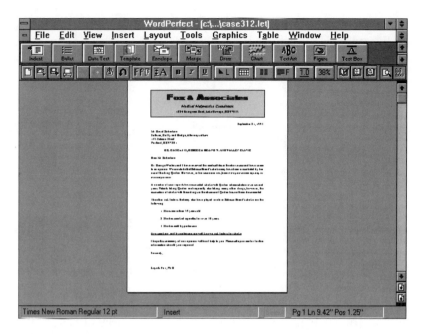

4. Click the Page Zoom button to return to regular Page view, and then click the Save button to save the letter before continuing.

The new margin settings are controlled by the margin codes in your document. If you are interested, take a look at these codes in the Reveal Codes area. (Click the codes to display their exact settings.) As you can see, WordPerfect has put Top Mar, Lft Mar, and Rgt Mar codes at the top of the document, and beginning and ending Rgt Mar Adj (for *right margin adjustment*) and Lft Mar Adj codes around the subject line to limit your margin adjustments to that one paragraph.

Predefining Formats

As you work with WordPerfect, you might notice that you use some types of formatting for all your documents. For example, you might always use full justification. Instead of having to change the formatting every time you start a new document, you can predefine a format so that every document is full-justified. Let's experiment by predefining a format for the other documents you'll create in this book:

1. Choose Document and then Initial Codes Style from the Layout menu to display the Styles Editor dialog box.

2. Choose Justification and then Full from the Style Editor's Layout menu. A Just code appears in the Contents box.

3. Click the Just code. As in the Reveal Codes area, the code expands to Just: Full, like this:

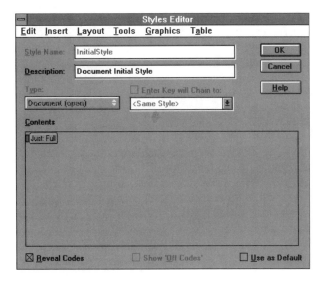

4. Click the Use As Default check box in the bottom-right corner of the dialog box to tell WordPerfect to apply this format to all future documents.

5. Click OK to return to the document window.

From now on, every document you create in WordPerfect will be full-justified. If you want to change the justification of a particular document, you can still do so by placing the insertion point at the beginning of the document and making the necessary selection from the Layout menu or the Power Bar.

Printing the Letter

Well, you now have an accurate, formatted letter ready for printing. Follow these steps:

1. Click the Page Zoom button to check that all your formatting is in place. Then click Page Zoom again.

2. Click the Print button on the Power Bar, and press Enter.

Be sure to save the letter because you'll use it again in the next chapter when you create letterhead templates.

Great-Looking Letterheads

4

What you will learn

*Add horizontal
and vertical lines
of various styles
and weights*

*Customize one of
WordPerfect's
templates to meet
your needs*

Fox & Associates
Medical Malpractice Consultants

1224 Evergreen Road ● Lake Oswego, OR 97035 ● (503) 555-4567

September 23, 1993

Mr. David Robertson
Sullivan, Duffy and Bridge,
145 Salmon Street
Portland, OR 97201

RE: CASE #31

Dear Mr. Robertson:

Dr. George Winters and I ha
opinion. We conclude that Re
Qnifen. However, in her case

A number of case reports ha
Patients taking Qnifen are fi
stroke with these drugs in th

The other risk factors that may

1. She is more than 59

2. She has smoked ciga

3. She has mild hypert

Age, smoking, and hypertens

I hope this summary of ou
information should you requ

Sincerely,

Kaye E. Fox, Ph.D.

Fox & Associates
Medical Malpractice Consultants

1224 Evergreen Road Lake Oswego, OR 97035 (503) 555-4567

September 23, 1993

Mr. David Robertson
Sullivan, Duffy and Bridge, Attorneys at Law
145 Salmon Street
Portland, OR 97201

RE: CASE #312, REBECCA BRAND V. MIDVALLEY CLINIC

Dear Mr. Robertson:

Dr. George Winters and I have reviewed the medical files in the above case and have come to an opinion. We conclude that Rebecca Brand's stroke may have been exacerbated by her use of the drug Qnifen. However, in her case *other risk factors may have been equally or more important*.

A number of case reports have associated stroke with Qnifen administration over several years. Patients taking Qnifen are frequently also taking many other drugs; however, the association of stroke with these drugs in the absence of Qnifen has not been documented.

The other risk factors that may also have played a role in Rebecca Brand's stroke are the following:

1. She is more than 59 years old.

2. She has smoked cigarettes for over 30 years.

3. She has mild hypertension.

Age, smoking, and hypertension are well-known risk factors for stroke.

I hope this summary of our opinion will be of help to you. Please call upon me for further information should you require it.

Sincerely,

Kaye E. Fox, Ph.D.

*Type text in
the template,
or merge an
existing file*

*Position text boxes
anywhere you
want them*

*Rotate text and adjust
alignment and margins
in the Text Editor*

*Frame the page with
simple or fancy page
borders*

Most businesses use letterhead stationery. The advantage of using a computer-generated letterhead is that you don't have to switch the paper in your printer from plain bond to letterhead every time you print a letter. In this chapter, we'll show you how to use the techniques you learned in Chapters 2 and 3 to modify one of the letterhead templates that is supplied with WordPerfect 6 for Windows. We'll also introduce you to some new features so that you can create your own letterhead. If you work for a company that already has preprinted letterhead, you probably have no choice about using it. However, you might want to use the instructions in this chapter to create a letterhead for your personal correspondence. As you follow along, you'll probably think of other ways you could put the letterhead techniques to work—for example, generating attractive flyers or eye-catching advertisements.

Customizing a Letterhead Template

First, we'll discuss the centered letterhead shown on the previous page. This letterhead is based on the LETTER3 template, which is supplied with WordPerfect. As you saw in Chapter 2, WordPerfect offers many different types of templates, from memos and letters to press releases and quarterly cash flow statements. You should explore WordPerfect's other templates on your own. You never know, one of them might be just right for the next document you plan to create.

Well, let's begin. If you're at the DOS prompt, type *win* to start the Windows program, and then double-click the WPWin 6.0 icon in the WPWin 6.0 group window to start WordPerfect. If you're already in WordPerfect, make sure your screen is clear (if necessary, choose New from the File menu). Then follow these steps:

Opening a template

1. If you added a Template button to the Button Bar in Chapter 1, click it now, or choose Template from the File menu to display the Templates dialog box. Then click the Options button, and select the Create Template option to display this dialog box:

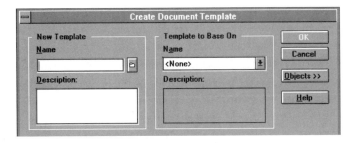

2. Type *lh1*—for *Letterhead 1*—in the Name edit box. (Word-Perfect automatically appends the template extension, WPT, to template filenames.) Then, in the Description edit box, type *Letterhead - With horizontal and vertical lines* as the letter-head template description. (Descriptions are optional, but they can help you recall what a particular template looks like.)

3. Finally, click the down arrow to the right of the Name option in the Template To Base On group box, select LETTER3 from the drop-down list, and click OK. WordPerfect displays this template:

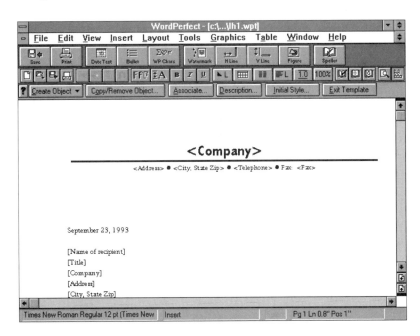

Because the new template is based on the LETTER3 template, the Button Bar changes to display the buttons WordPerfect thinks you are most likely to use with this template. Notice also that the Template Feature Bar now appears below the Power Bar.

The Template Feature Bar

4. Double-click *<Company>* to select the entire word, type *Fox & Associates*, and press Enter to start a new line.

5. Type *Medical Malpractice Consultants* under the company name. Don't worry about these words appearing below the horizontal line. We'll fix that in a moment.

6. To center *Medical Malpractice Consultants*, display the Justification pop-up list on the Power Bar, and select Center.

Now fill in the rest of the letterhead:

1. Double-click *<Address>* to select it, and type *1224 Evergreen Road* followed by a space. Then select *<City, State Zip>*, type *Lake Oswego, OR 97035*, select *<Telephone>*, and type *(503) 555-4567*. We are not going to include a Fax number (although you're welcome to add your own), so with the insertion point placed just after the telephone number, press Shift+End to select to the end of the line, and press Delete.

2. Save your work by clicking the Save button on the Power Bar (or the Button Bar).

As you learned in Chapter 2, when you use templates, it's important to consider exactly how much information the templates must contain in order to meet your needs. For example, you might want to use the letterhead template for something other than letters, such as flyers and press releases. In these cases, you would not want to include the return address, salutation, and so on. Later in the chapter, we'll merge the LH1.WPT template with the letter you created in Chapter 3. In this case, the letter already contains a return address, salutation, and closing, so we can delete those items from the template. Follow these steps:

1. Click an insertion point just before *[Name of recipient]*, scroll the document until *<Title>* comes into view, hold down the Shift key, and click after *<Title>* to select everything below the date.

2. Press Delete to delete the selected text, press Ctrl+Home to move to the top of the document, and then click the Save button on the Power Bar (or the Button Bar).

Selecting beyond the screen

You can select text that extends beyond the reaches of your screen by holding down the left mouse button and then dragging to the edge of the screen in the direction you want to select. The document scrolls as you continue to hold down the mouse button. Release the button when you've selected the desired text.

Creating and Editing Lines

WordPerfect is extremely versatile when it comes to creating and editing lines. Let's change the horizontal line in the letterhead template and then add a vertical line so that you can see what we mean. First, reposition the horizontal line in LH1.WPT, and then change its style by following these steps:

1. Move the insertion point to the end of the *Medical Malpractice Consultants* line, and press Enter to add a blank line so that you have more room to work.

2. Point to the horizontal line, and when the mouse pointer changes from an I-beam to an arrow, click the left mouse button to select the line. WordPerfect surrounds the line with small black squares called *handles*:

Selecting lines

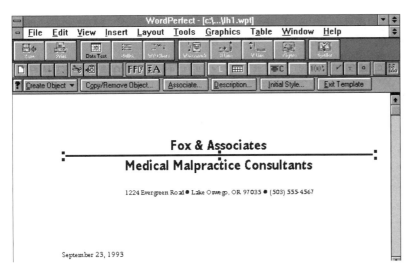

3. To reposition the line below *Medical Malpractice Consultants*, move the mouse pointer over the selected line (the pointer changes to a four-headed arrow), hold down the left mouse button, and drag the line downward. Release the mouse button when the line is where you want it.

Moving lines

Now let's fine-tune the line's position a bit and then change its style:

1. Choose the Edit Line command from the Graphics menu to display the dialog box shown on the next page.

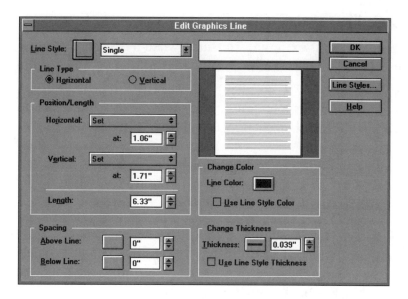

WordPerfect displays the settings for the horizontal line. The page diagram on the right side of the dialog box shows the current position of the line relative to the page. (If your document contains more than one line, be sure to select the line you want to work with before choosing the Edit Line command.)

2. In the Position/Length group box, change the Vertical setting to *1.70* by typing directly in the At edit box or by clicking the arrowheads to the right of the At edit box.

Changing line styles

3. Now click the arrow to the right of the Line Style option box to display a drop-down list of line styles. (You can also click the sample box to the left of the Line Style option box to display samples of all the available line styles with the current selection highlighted.) Click the Triple line style to select it. WordPerfect displays a sample of the selected line style in the box at the top of the Edit Graphics Line dialog box.

4. Select the Use Line Style Thickness option in the Change Thickness group box so that WordPerfect will use the Triple line style as the basis for determining the thickness of the line. Then click OK to return to the template, which now looks like this:

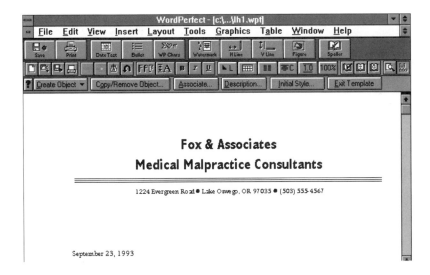

To add the vertical line shown in the sample letterhead at the beginning of the chapter, follow these steps:

1. Click the Vertical Line button on the Button Bar. Instantly a vertical line appears on the left side of the document window.

2. Change the vertical line's style and position by first selecting it with the mouse and then choosing the Edit Line command from the Graphics menu.

3. Select Double from the Line Style drop-down list.

4. In the Position/Length group box, select Set from the Horizontal pop-up list, and then type *0.75* in the At edit box to position the line three-quarters of an inch from the left edge of the page.

5. Click OK to return to the document window.

Now lengthen the horizontal lines so that they intersect the vertical lines:

1. Click the horizontal "line" to select it.

2. Point to the middle handle at the left end of the line, and when the pointer changes to a double-headed arrow, hold down the left mouse button, and drag to the left until the line extends about one-half inch into the document's left margin, as shown on the next page.

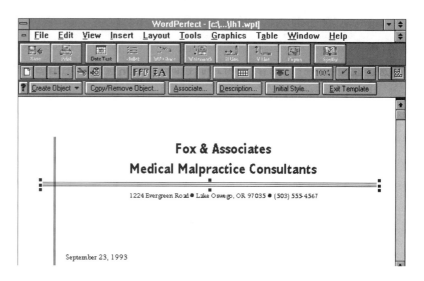

Watermarks

Watermarks are logos, graphics, or display type that appear "behind" the printed text of your document. (Diplomas and stock certificates often sport watermarks.) You can use Word-Perfect's Watermark feature to create your own stationery or to dress up other documents. Simply choose Watermark from the Layout menu, and click Create in the Watermark dialog box. (You can have up to two different watermarks—A and B—in a document.) Then use the Watermark Feature Bar as well as Word-Perfect's commands and buttons to create a watermark. For example, click the Figure button on the Watermark Feature Bar, and select one of WordPerfect's graphics from the Insert Image dialog box. Then click Close on both the Graphics Box Feature Bar and the Watermark Feature Bar to return to the document window, where you can enter the text of your document. (For more information about graphics, see Chapter 6.)

Final Touches

Because WordPerfect supports so many fonts, you can really have fun experimenting with different effects in your documents. Before you test print the new letterhead template, let's change the font of the company name to make it a bit more dramatic:

1. Select *Fox & Associates*, and then choose Font from the Layout menu.

2. In the Font dialog box, select a new font from the Font Face list box and a size from the Font Size list box, and check the results in the sample box. Continue selecting fonts until you find one you like, and then click OK. The font and size we selected—Swis721 BlkEx BT Bold 30pt—is shown at the beginning of the chapter.

3. Next select *Medical Malpractice Consultants*, choose Font from the Layout menu, and select the same font in a smaller size—we chose Swis721 BlkEx BT Regular 14pt.

Finally, let's close up the space between the letterhead and the date:

1. Click an insertion point at the beginning of the date, and press Backspace three times.

2. Save your changes.

Test Printing

It's always a good idea to test print a document that you plan to use as a template. That way, you can determine whether or not you need to make any adjustments before you actually use the template. As you've already seen, printing in Word-Perfect is a simple two-step process:

1. Click the Print button on the Power Bar (or the Button Bar).

2. When the Print dialog box appears, click Print to send the template file to the printer.

Take a moment to admire your efforts.

Merging the Letterhead with a Letter

Now we're ready to merge the letterhead with a letter. In this section, we'll load the letter we created in Chapter 3 and then merge the LH1.WPT document at the top. Before we merge the new letterhead, we'll delete the existing letterhead and date from the letter. Follow these steps:

1. Clear the document window by clicking the Exit Template button on the Template Bar. WordPerfect locks in the changes you have made to the template so that you can use it as the basis for new documents, just like the templates that shipped with the program. (If you want to make changes to the template later, simply select the template in the Templates dialog box, and then select the Edit Template option in the Options drop-down list.)

Saving and closing templates

2. Click the Open button on the Power Bar, and when the Open File dialog box appears, double-click the CASE312.LET file to open it.

3. Hold down the Shift key, and click to the left of the *M* in *Mr. David Robertson* to select the letterhead and the date. Your screen should look like the one on the next page.

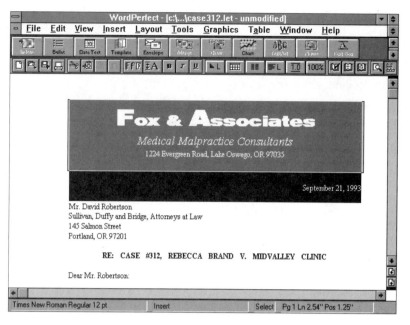

Have you wondered about the QuickList option in many of WordPerfect's dialog boxes, such as Open File and Save As? You can set up QuickList so that you can quickly access the files and directories you use most often. Simply choose any command whose resulting dialog box offers the QuickList option, such as the Open command on the File menu. When the dialog box appears, click the QuickList option, and select Show QuickList to display the QuickList box in the active dialog box. Next select the Add Item option from the QuickList drop-down list, and enter a full pathname and description for the files or directories you want to include in the QuickList. When you use a dialog box that requires you to enter a filename or directory, you can then quickly select the file or directory from the Quick-List. If you want to redisplay the Directories list, select Show Directories or Show Both from the QuickList drop-down list. You can also edit and delete items in the QuickList by using the corresponding options in the QuickList drop-down list.

4. Press the Delete key to delete the selected text.

5. Now save the changes to the letter by clicking the Save button on the Power Bar.

With the old letterhead and date deleted, you're ready to merge the new letterhead with the letter:

1. Be sure the insertion point is at the top of the letter, where the letterhead will be inserted.

2. Choose File from the Insert menu to display this dialog box:

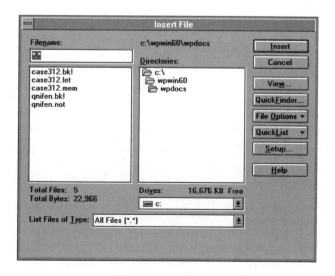

3. Double-click the WPWIN60 directory in the Directories list box, and then double-click the TEMPLATE subdirectory to display the template files.

The TEMPLATE subdirectory

4. Scroll to LH1.WPT in the list of files, and double-click it.

5. When WordPerfect asks whether you want to insert the file in the current document, click Yes. Here's the result:

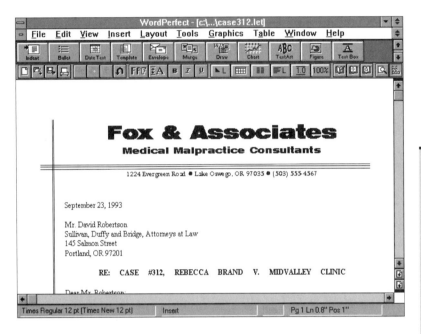

6. Check that everything is in place by clicking the Page Zoom button on the Power Bar.

Notice that the letter is no longer full-justified. Follow the steps below to correct this minor problem:

1. With Page Zoom mode still active, click an insertion point to the left of the *D* in *Dear Mr. Robertson*, and select Full from the Justification pop-up list on the Power Bar.

2. Now choose Save As from the File menu. When the Save As dialog box appears, return to the WPDOCS directory by first double-clicking the WPWIN60 directory in the Directories list box and then double-clicking the WPDOCS directory. Save the merged letter with a different filename—perhaps, *case312.lh1*—so that you can use the unmerged letter later.

3. Clear the window by choosing Close from the File menu.

Document summaries

You can attach a document summary to your document by choosing Document Summary from the File menu and filling in the appropriate information in the Document Summary dialog box. You can enter general information about your document, such as a descriptive name, revision date, author, and so on, that you can use later to help organize and locate the document file (see the tip about QuickFinder on page 35). Use the Configure and Options buttons in the Document Summary dialog box to change the summary fields, extract information from the document, and print, delete, or save the summary as a separate document. You can automatically attach summaries to all your documents by choosing Preferences from the File menu, double-clicking the Summary icon in the Preferences dialog box, and selecting Create Summary On Save/Exit.

Now let's print the merged letter, this time from the Open File dialog box:

Printing from the Open File dialog box

1. Click the Open button on the Power Bar to display the Open File dialog box.

2. Select the CASE312.LH1 file, click File Options to display a drop-down list of options, and select Print.

3. When the Print File dialog box appears, check that the correct path and filename are displayed in the File To Print edit box, and then click the Print button. (If necessary, you can type the path and filename in the File To Print edit box.)

4. Click the Cancel button to close the dialog box in preparation for the next letterhead.

Creating a Letterhead from Scratch

The letterhead you just created does the job, but it's very simple. Let's explore some of the WordPerfect features that can help you create a more sophisticated letterhead. As you follow along, refer to the second sample letterhead pictured at the beginning of the chapter so that you can see the effect you are aiming for. Again, you can use the sample name and address or substitute your own.

As with the first letterhead template, we must designate the new letterhead document as a template so that it can be used repeatedly. Follow these steps:

1. Click the Template button or choose Template from the File menu, and select Create Template from the Options drop-down list.

2. Type *lh2* as the template name, and click OK. (We're creating this template from scratch, so this time we won't base it on an existing template.) WordPerfect displays the Template Feature Bar across the blank document window.

3. Whoops! We forgot to enter a description. No problem: We can easily enter one from the document window. Click the Description button on the Template Bar, type *Letterhead - With border and vertical box*, and click OK.

File management

You can use the options available in the File Options drop-down list to copy files to other directories, rename and delete files, print the current file list, and remove an existing directory. You can even change the status of a file's "protective attributes" by selecting Change Attributes from the File Options drop-down list, and then selecting or deselecting the appropriate attributes. (Archive tells third-party backup programs that the file has changed since the last backup; Read-Only protects the file from deletion or modification; Hidden hides the file in dialog box file lists and in the QuickFinder Search Results list; System designates the file as part of your computer's operating system.) In addition, you can use the Setup option in the Open File dialog box (and related dialog boxes) to change the display of files in the file list or to sort the list by filename, extension, size, date and time of creation, or descriptive name or type. (You can add a descriptive name and type in the Document Summary dialog box; see the tip on page 77.)

Now we can lay the groundwork for the new letterhead. The first step is to create the border that appears around the perimeter of the page:

1. Decrease all four margins by choosing Margins from the Layout menu and setting the Left, Right, Top, and Bottom margins to *0.25*.

2. Choose Page and then Border/Fill from the Layout menu to display the Page Border dialog box. Select Hairline from the Border Style drop-down list, and click OK. (As with line styles, you can click the sample box to the left of the Border Style option box to display samples of all the available border styles with the current selection highlighted.)

Adding a page border

Now we need to insert the text box that will contain the text of the letterhead. As the name implies, a text box contains an insertion point so that you can enter and format text directly in it. Follow these steps:

1. Click the Text Box button on the Button Bar. WordPerfect inserts a text box that looks like this:

Inserting a text box

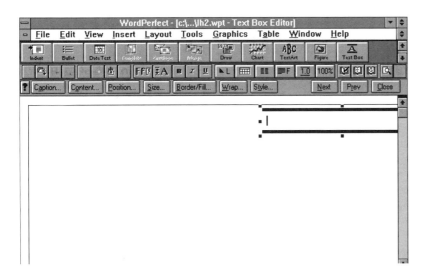

The title bar indicates that the Text Box Editor is currently active. You can move around the Text Box Editor just as you move around the normal document window, and you can use many of the same menu commands and buttons. Notice that WordPerfect has replaced the Template Feature Bar with the Graphics Box Feature Bar. As you'll see, you can use the

Graphics Box Bar to manipulate text boxes in various ways. (In Chapter 6, you'll use the buttons on this feature bar to work with graphics.)

Entering text in a text box

2. In the text box, type *Fox & Associates*, and press Enter. On the second line, type *Medical Malpractice Consultants*, and press Enter.

3. Type the last line of the letterhead, *1224 Evergreen Road Lake Oswego, OR 97035   (503) 555-4567*, inserting two spaces between *Evergreen Road* and *Lake Oswego* and between the ZIP code and the telephone number. Don't worry about bad breaks or strange word spacing; we'll take care of that later.

4. Click the Position button on the Graphics Box Bar to display this dialog box:

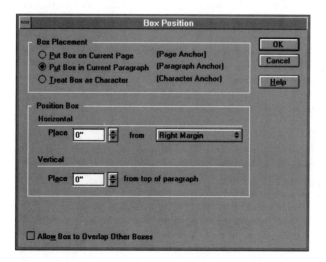

5. Select the Put Box On Current Page option, and click OK. Now the text box is anchored to the page rather than attached to the first paragraph of the template.

Before we go any further, here are a few pointers about working with text boxes and the Text Box Editor:

• To deactivate the Text Box Editor, click anywhere outside the currently selected text box.

- To activate the Text Box Editor, double-click anywhere inside the text box.

- To choose the commands that are applicable to text boxes, right-click the text box to display its QuickMenu.

- To remove the Graphics Box Bar, click its Close button.

- To display the Graphics Box Bar, right-click the text box, and choose Feature Bar from the QuickMenu.

  With that out of the way, let's concentrate on changing the text box's size and adding a border:

1. Be sure the Text Box Editor is still active (check the title bar), and then click the Size button on the Graphics Box Bar to display the Box Size dialog box shown here:

Changing the text box's size

2. Change the Width setting by double-clicking the current setting in the Set edit box and typing *1.35*.

3. Change the Height setting by simply selecting the Full option. Then click OK to return to the Text Box Editor.

  Now we'll add a border so that the text box is easier to see:

1. Click the Border/Fill button on the Graphics Box Bar to display the Box Border/Fill Styles dialog box, and select Hairline from the Border Style drop-down list.

Adding a border

2. Next click the Customize Style button to display the dialog box shown on the next page.

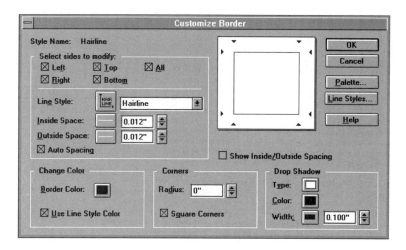

You can use the Customize Border dialog box to change the entire border or specific sides of the border, to change the color of the border (see the tip on page 85), to round the corners, and to add a drop shadow (both discussed on page 143). We'll use this dialog box to add a little buffer space between the letterhead and any letters that we merge later.

Adding buffer space

3. Double-click the setting in the Outside Space edit box, and type *0.2*. Then click OK twice to return to the Text Box Editor.

To reposition the text box on the page, you use the same techniques that you used to move the horizontal and vertical lines in the first letterhead. Follow these steps:

Moving the text box

1. Point to the text box's border, and when the pointer changes to a four-headed arrow, hold down the mouse button, and drag the text box to the left side of the page, as far as it will go.

2. Fine-tune the text box's position by clicking the Position button on the Graphics Box Bar, typing *6.70* in the Horizontal Place edit box, and clicking OK. Then click anywhere outside the text box to deactivate the Text Box Editor.

As you continue to work with WordPerfect's text box and graphics features, you'll find that you often have to make several adjustments to achieve the right effect. For example, now that we've repositioned the text box, it no longer fits neatly inside the page border. Resize the text box manually by following these steps:

1. Select the text box. (Notice that when the text box is selected in the document window, WordPerfect dims many of the commands and buttons, indicating that they cannot be used.)

2. Point to any handle at the top of the text box (you may have to scroll to the top of the page), and when the pointer changes to a double-headed arrow, drag the box up or down so that it aligns with the top of the page border.

Manually adjusting the text box's size

3. If necessary, repeat this step for the bottom of the text box. Then click the document window to deselect the text box, and save the template.

Now let's do something about the letterhead text. We'll move it to the top of the text box and rotate it 90 degrees counter-clockwise, and then we'll add a little formatting, like this:

1. Double-click the text box to activate the Text Box Editor, and then click the Content button on the Graphics Box Bar to display the dialog box shown here:

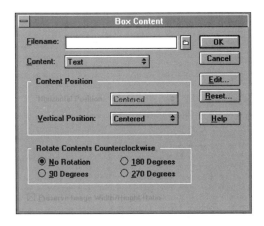

Note that you can use the Filename edit box in the Box Content dialog box to insert an existing text file into the selected text box.

2. Select Top from the Vertical Position pop-up list, and then select 90 Degrees from the Rotate Contents Counterclockwise group box.

Repositioning and rotating text in a text box

3. Click the Edit button to return to the Text Box Editor. Because you have rotated the text, the Text Box Editor displays the text in a special window like the one shown on the next page.

Editing rotated text

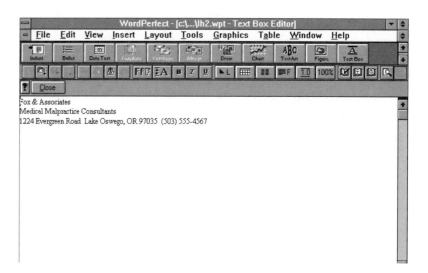

TextArt

If you want to add a touch of whimsy to your letterhead, or if you need a special artsy look for a brochure or flyer, try Word-Perfect's new TextArt feature, which enables you to create special effects with text. Click the TextArt button on the Button Bar to display the TextArt window. Then type your text, and select a shape to "pour" the text into. You can specify a text color, an outline weight and color, and a fill pattern by clicking their respective buttons and selecting from the available options. You can also specify the angle of rotation and width and height of the text. When the text in the sample box looks the way you want it, choose Exit & Return To WordPerfect from the File menu. WordPerfect asks whether you want to update the embedded object in your document. Click Yes to embed the text as a TextArt graphic. To edit the text after embedding, double-click it to redisplay it in the TextArt window, where you can adjust it to your heart's content.

4. With the insertion point at the beginning of the text, select Right from the Justification pop-up list on the Power Bar.

5. Without moving the insertion point, choose Font from the Layout menu, select Humanst521 Cn BT, click Bold in the Font Style list, select 36 from the Font Size list, and click OK.

6. Then move the insertion point to the beginning of the second line of the letterhead, and select 18 from the Font Size drop-down list on the Power Bar.

7. Click the Close button to return to the document window, and then press Ctrl+Home. The letterhead now looks like this:

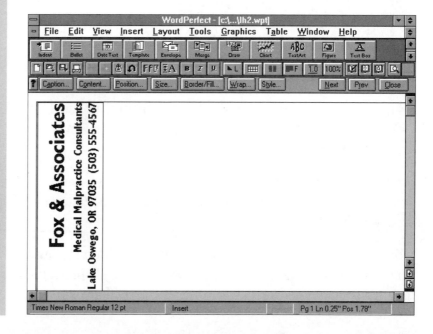

8. Save the letterhead by clicking the Save button.

The text of the letterhead and the top border of the text box are a little too close for comfort. We can easily correct this problem by increasing the right margin. Yes, the *right* margin, not the *top* margin. Because we rotated the text 90 degrees counterclockwise, what appears to be the top margin is actually the right margin. Follow the steps below to make the margin adjustment:

1. Double-click the text box to activate the Text Box Editor.

2. With the insertion point at the beginning of the letterhead, choose Margins from the Layout menu.

3. In the Margins dialog box, type *0.5* in the Right edit box, and click OK. Then click the Close button to return to the document window.

WordPerfect not only offers you a wide range of choices for putting borders around text, but as you saw in Chapter 3, you can also fill the space between borders with a variety of patterns or shading. Let's finish up this letterhead by adding a fill pattern to the text box:

1. Select the text box with the mouse, and click the Border/Fill button on the Graphics Box Bar.

2. In the Box Border/Fill Styles dialog box, select Diagonal Lines 1 from the Fill Style drop-down list.

3. Click the Foreground option to display a color palette, and select the light gray color (ninth from the left).

4. Click OK to return to the document window. You can see the result in the illustration at the beginning of the chapter.

5. Click Close to remove the Graphics Box Bar.

Before moving on to the next section, let's insert a Date code at the top of the letterhead. When you include a Date code in a document, WordPerfect automatically inserts the current date (from your system clock) at the location of the code every time you load or print the document. Follow the steps on the next page.

Colorific!

WordPerfect offers a whole host of colors that can be used for text, borders, fill, and anything else that appears in the document window. All you have to do is click the Color box in the corresponding dialog box, such as the Font or Customize Border dialog box, and select a color from the available color palette. Even if you don't have a color printer, it's fun to experiment with the color palette. And if you're not satisfied with the current palette, you can change to a different one or create your own. Choose Font from the Layout menu, and click the Palette option at the bottom of the Font dialog box to display the Define Color Printing Palette dialog box. Click the Open option to select a different palette or use the color wheel and color models to define a new palette. You can use the options below the color palette to change the palette's size, to copy a color and paste it over another, to blend colors, to create a spectrum of colors, or to invert the selected color. After you've defined your color palette, click Save As, and give your palette a name. You can always switch to a different palette by using the Open option, and you can return to the default palette by clicking the Default option. Finally, you can display the colors in the color palette in list form by selecting the Show As List option at the top of the dialog box. (You can even assign names to the colors in the list by selecting a color and then entering a name for it in the Name edit box.)

Inserting the current date

1. Click an insertion point at the top of the document, choose Date and Date Code from the Insert menu, and press Enter.

2. Save the letterhead template by clicking the Exit Template button on the Template Bar. When WordPerfect asks whether you want to save your changes, click Yes.

Copying One Document into Another

You've already seen how you can use the File command on the Insert menu to merge two files. This time we'll use another method to combine the letterhead and a letter. In the process, we'll practice working with more than one document window. (As we mentioned in Chapter 1, you can have up to nine windows open at a time.) Follow these steps:

1. Click the Open button on the Power Bar, and double-click CASE312.LET to open the letter file.

Using the new template

2. Open a new document based on the LH2.WPT template by clicking the Template button on the Button Bar or choosing Template from the File menu and then double-clicking LH2 in the Document Template To Use list box.

3. Now activate CASE312.LET by choosing it from the Window menu, and then choose the Tile command from the Window menu to display both document windows at once.

With CASE312.LET and a document based on the LH2 template displayed in their respective windows, we can copy and paste the letter from one window to the other, like this:

1. Click an insertion point to the left of the *M* in *Mr. David Robertson*, scroll to the end of the document, hold down Shift, and click after *Ph.D.*

2. Click the Copy button on the Power Bar.

3. Now click the Document2 window to make it active, press Ctrl+End, and then press Enter twice to add some space.

4. Click the Paste button on the Power Bar to place the copy of the letter at the insertion point in the letterhead template.

5. Save the merged document in the WPDOCS directory with an appropriate name, such as *case312.lh2.*

6. Click the CASE312.LET window to activate it, and then double-click its Control menu (the box with the dash at the left end of the window's title bar) to close the window.

7. Expand the CASE312.LH2 window by clicking its Maximize button, and press Ctrl+Home to move to the top of the document. Your screen now looks like this:

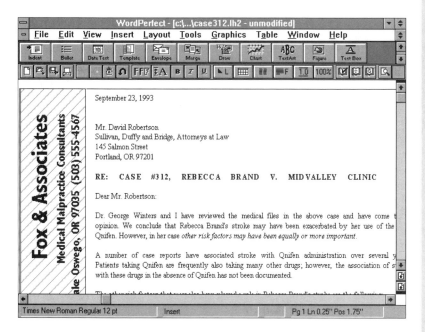

Notice anything wrong? The margins of the letter have changed to reflect the current setting for the letterhead, which is 0.25 inch for the left, right, top, and bottom margins. Here's how to fix this problem:

1. Select the text of the letter, excluding the date. Choose Paragraph and then Format from the Layout menu to display the Paragraph Format dialog box. Type *1* in the Right Margin Adjustment edit box, and click OK.

2. Now move the text down from the top of the page. Click an insertion point before the date, and choose Typesetting and then Advance from the Layout menu to display the dialog box shown on the next page.

Window treatments

You can manipulate document windows by using the commands on the *document* Control menu (not to be confused with the *application* Control menu—see page 2). When a window is maximized, you can choose Restore from the Control menu to restore the window to its previous size. Use the Move and Size commands in conjunction with the Arrow keys to move and resize the active window. Press Enter to lock in any changes in the window's location or size. (You can also move a document window by clicking its title bar and dragging with the mouse, and you can resize a window by positioning the mouse pointer over one of the window's frames, and dragging the double-arrow pointer in the desired direction.) Choose Minimize to reduce the window to an icon and Maximize to restore the window to full size. When a window is reduced to an icon, you can restore the window's previous size by double-clicking the icon, or you can click the icon once to display the Control menu, and then choose Maximize. Use the Close and Next commands to close the active window and to switch to the next open window, respectively.

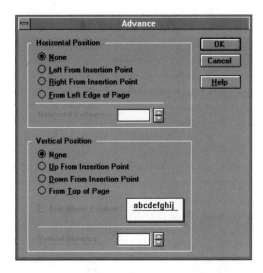

3. Select the Down From Insertion Point option, type *1* in the
   Vertical Distance edit box, and click OK.

4. Print the document, which should be identical to the letter at
   the beginning of the chapter. Then choose Close from the File
   menu, and when WordPerfect asks if you want to save your
   changes, click Yes.

Creating a Directory for the Letters

Without leaving WordPerfect, you can organize your files by
creating directories for specific types of documents and then
moving or copying your files to the new directories. For
example, you can create a directory called *LETTERS* for your
letters. (Directory names must be eight or fewer characters.)
Take a few minutes to do that now:

1. Click the Open button on the Power Bar.

2. In the Open File dialog box, click File Options, and select
   Create Directory. WordPerfect displays this dialog box:

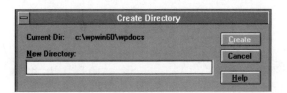

3. Type the full pathname of the new directory in the New Directory edit box (we typed *c:\wpwin60\wpdocs\letters*), and

press Enter. The new directory appears as a subdirectory of WPDOCS in the Directories list box.

Now move the letter files:

1. Select the CASE312.LH1 file, and then select Move from the File Options drop-down list to display this dialog box:

Moving files to a new directory

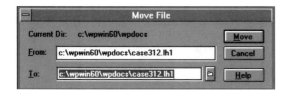

2. In the To edit box, type the pathname of the file in its new directory (we typed *c:\wpwin60\wpdocs\letters\case312.lh1*). You can also edit the existing pathname in the To edit box by clicking an insertion point after *wpdocs* and typing *\letters*. Then click the Move button to move the file.

3. Repeat steps 1 and 2 to move CASE312.LH2.

4. To be sure that the letter files really were moved to the new directory, double-click the LETTERS directory in the Directories list box. Here they are:

Displaying files in a directory

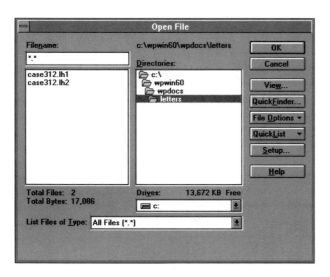

5. Now double-click WPDOCS in the Directories list box to return to that directory.

That's all there is to creating directories!

5

Professional Reports

What you will learn

Apply built-in styles or create your own for speedy formatting

See headers and footers in place on the screen as you create them

DRUG-INDUCED STROKE

Risk Factors

A number of important health
in humans. These include:

Age: The incidence of stroke
in young individuals. A sharp i
of age.

Hypertension: The risk of stro
blood pressure. It has now b
major factor in reducing the i
is diagnosed and treated, the

Smoking: Smoking is a well-es
more they have smoked, the
cessation of smoking at any t
of coronary disease and heart a
but in all likelihood the same

Diabetes: Diabetes and some
of stroke. Diabetics who do no
Whether strict control of di
reduces the risk of stroke is

Drugs

Three classes of drugs used t
with stroke.

Drugs That Stimulate Blood P
cocaine. Adrenalin is used ther
are commonly abused for the

- Increase blood pr
- Increase heart rat
- Stimulate brain

Drugs That Damage Blood Vessels: A few drugs used for long periods of time can damage blood vessels, which weakens their walls and, in the case of arteries in the brain, may lead to stroke. How these drugs produce this effect is not clear, but it is thought that it occurs in the following steps:

1. With continual administration over long periods of time, the drug accumulates in the cells that line the artery.

2. As the drug accumulates, it gradually inhibits the cells' metabolic processes.

3. Eventually, the cells of the artery die, leaving the vessel wall weakened and vulnerable.

Qnifen and Fiszol: Both of these drugs are used to treat osteoporosis (softening of the bone). Both have also been associated with stroke, but to varying degrees. A summary description of the drugs is given below:

Qnifen was the first drug developed for the treatment of osteoporosis. However, after several years of use, it became associated with stroke.

Fiszol was recently approved for the treatment of osteoporosis. Because Fiszol has a different structure than Qnifen, current theory is that Fiszol will not have the same side effects. However, clinical trials have not yet corroborated this theory.

Although both Qnifen and Fiszol appear to be equally effective in treating osteoporosis, they differ greately in their chemical structures. While Qnifen contains one methyl group (CH_3), Fiszol has none. This structural difference may explain why patients taking Qnifen have a higher incidence of stroke than patients taking Fiszol. The following statement was recently published in the *New World Journal of Medicine*:

Early reports of fewer cases of stroke associated with Fiszol would indicate that at this time, Fiszol is a better choice than Qnifen in the treatment of osteoporosis.[1]

---

[1]R. Urban, "Fiszol versus Qnifen and Stroke." New World Journal of Medicine, 217:312-315, 1993.

Combine custom tabs and indents to get exactly the look you want

Create bulleted lists with ease using the Bullets & Numbers feature

Customize the look and location of page numbers

Document your sources with easy-to-create footnotes

In many professions, writing reports is a common task. Whether you're a scientist, an administrative assistant, a marketing specialist, or an attorney, WordPerfect for Windows can help take the drudgery out of report writing. In this chapter, we'll introduce you to WordPerfect's features for creating outlines, styles, lists, parallel columns, and footnotes. In addition, we'll show you how to add headers and numbers to your pages.

To demonstrate these features, we need to work with a document that is longer than those we created in previous chapters. You can either create a report of your own or use the one shown on the previous page. In the following sections, you type just enough text to use the feature we are discussing. You can refer to the illustrations on the previous page to see how all these features can be combined to create a useful report.

Outlining Documents

Different people work in different ways. Some people launch right into a project, starting at the beginning and working their way through in a linear fashion until they've crossed the last *t* and dotted the last *i*. Others depend heavily on outlines, creating an overview of the project and then filling in the details. If you fall into the latter category, this section is for you. Although the report we're writing is relatively short, it contains enough headings to give you a good idea of how WordPerfect's Outline feature works. Follow these steps to see how easy it is to create an outline in WordPerfect:

1. With a clear document window, choose the Outline command from the Tools menu. As you can see at the top of the next page, WordPerfect turns on the Outline Feature Bar, inserts a 1 followed by a period and a tab, and indicates that this is a first level heading by displaying a hollow 1 to the left of the number. For good measure, WordPerfect also displays *Level 1* in the status bar.

The Outline Feature Bar

2. Click the down arrow to the right of the word *Paragraph* on the Outline Bar, and select Outline from the drop-down list

Changing the outline style

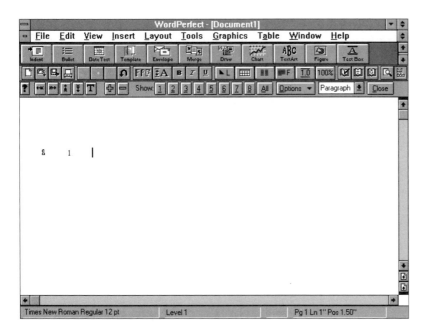

of available outline styles. WordPerfect changes the 1 to a Roman numeral I.

3. Choose Reveal Codes from the View menu. In the Reveal Codes area, notice that WordPerfect has inserted an Outline code, a Para Style code, and a Style code at the beginning of the document. Every time you press Enter while creating an outline, WordPerfect inserts a Para Style code after the hard return to identify the outline level and a Style code to control the numbering system. Choose Reveal Codes again to close the Reveal Codes area.

Now create the outline, using the Backspace or Delete key if you make a mistake:

1. Press the Caps Lock key, type *DRUG-INDUCED STROKE*, and then press Enter to start a new entry. WordPerfect inserts II at the beginning of the line.

2. Press the Tab key to change to level two. The insertion point moves over one tab, A replaces II, the level indicator to the left changes to a hollow 2, and the level 1 indicator for the preceding line acquires a plus (+) sign to indicate that it has sublevels. Press the Caps Lock key to turn off capitalization,

Custom outline styles

If you need a custom outline, you can either edit an existing outline definition or create an entirely new one. Click Options on the Outline Feature Bar, and select Define Outline from the drop-down list. In the Outline Define dialog box, click the Edit button to edit an existing definition or the Create button to create a new one. You can then set up the levels to appear exactly as you want them, including indents, numbers or bullets, and styles. If you want the custom outline definition to be available for other documents, you can copy it to a template.

type *Drugs*, and press Enter to start a new line. WordPerfect inserts B at the beginning of the line.

3. Press Tab to change to level three. The insertion point moves over one more tab, 1 replaces B, the level indicator changes to a hollow 3, and the preceding level 2 indicator acquires a plus sign.

4. Type *Drugs That Stimulate Blood Pressure:* (be sure to include the colon), and press Enter to start a new line. WordPerfect inserts a 2 at the beginning of the line.

5. Type *Drugs That Damage Blood Vessels:*, and press Enter to start a new line.

6. Press Shift+Tab to change from level three to level two. The insertion point moves back one tab, B replaces 3, and the level indicator changes to 2. Type *Qnifen and Fiszol*, and press Enter to start a new line.

7. Type *Risk Factors,* and press Enter again to start a new line.

8. Press Tab to change to level three, and type four more entries for *Age:*, *Hypertension:*, *Smoking:*, and *Diabetes:*, but don't press Enter after *Diabetes.*

Ending the outline → 9. Now click the Options button on the Outline Bar, and select End Outline to turn off outlining. (Notice that WordPerfect automatically inserts another line in your document, designating it with a T for *text*.) The outline now looks like this:

Outline Button Bar

When working with outlines, you might want to turn on the Outline Button Bar by right-clicking the current Button Bar and choosing Outline from the QuickMenu. The Outline Button Bar provides six buttons that quickly accomplish such tasks as accessing the Outline Define dialog box, changing outline levels, and selecting paragraphs and families.

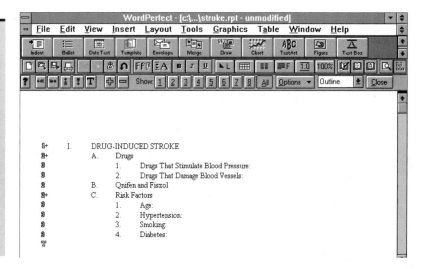

10. Choose Save As from the File menu, and save the outline in the C:\WPWIN60\WPDOCS directory with the filename *stroke.rpt*. Then click the Print button on the Power Bar, and print the outline.

Viewing and Editing Outlines

Outlines are great for organizing your thoughts. It is a rare person who can create a perfect outline right off the bat, and most people have to spend some time organizing and reorganizing topics. WordPerfect's Outline feature enables you to see the structure of documents at any level of detail you choose, and it lets you move things around to your heart's content, searching for the most logical order. Let's take a brief look at some of these capabilities:

1. Move the insertion point to the beginning of the outline, and click the Show 2 button on the Outline Bar to display only the level one and level two entries, like this:

Displaying selected levels

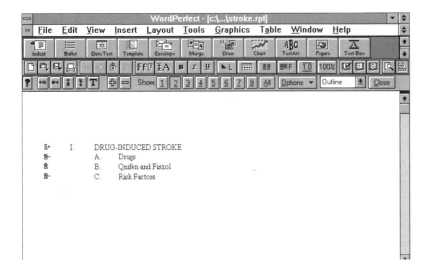

2. Move the insertion point to the first second-level entry (*Drugs*), and click the Show Family button on the Outline Bar to redisplay the level three entries under *Drugs*. (A *family* is an entry and its subentries.)

Displaying a specific family

3. Repeat step 2 for the *Risk Factors* entry. (To once again hide these entries, you can simply click the Hide Family button— the one with the fat minus sign—on the Outline Bar.)

Hiding a specific family

Changing levels

4. Move the insertion point to the *Qnifen and Fiszol* entry, and on the Outline Bar, click the Next Level button to change the entry level from two to three. (Clicking the Previous Level button—the one with the left-pointing arrow—does the opposite.) Notice that *Risk Factors* is renumbered from C to B.

5. Press the End key, and type a colon to make the *Qnifen and Fiszol* entry consistent with the other third level entries.

Now for a little rearranging:

Selecting a family

1. Click the 2+ indicator to the left of the *Risk Factors* entry to select the entire family (the *Risk Factors* entry and all its subentries).

Moving a family

2. Point to the family's 2+ indicator. When the pointer changes to a double-headed arrow, hold down the left mouse button, and drag upward until the line indicator is above the *Drugs* entry. When you release the mouse button, WordPerfect moves the *Risk Factors* family and automatically renumbers the outline entries, as shown here:

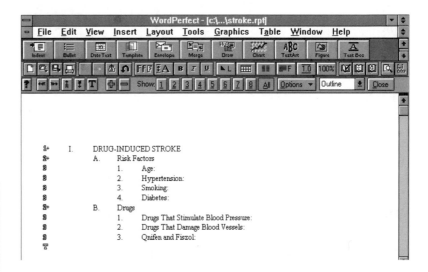

> **Moving entries with buttons**
>
> After selecting an entry or a family, you can move it up or down in the outline by clicking the Move Up and Move Down buttons (the buttons with the up and down arrows) on the Outline Feature Bar.

Let's add a little text to the outline:

1. Move the insertion point to the end of the *Risk Factors* entry, and then press Enter. WordPerfect creates another level two entry, labeled B.

2. For the new entry, type the following:

   A number of important health conditions are now recognized as contributing to the cause of stroke in humans. These include:

3. With the insertion point located in the new text, click the Body Text button on the Outline Bar to change the entry to normal body text. (If you click the Next Level or Previous Level button on the Outline Bar, the text reverts to an outline level.)

   T

   Changing entries to body text

4. Press Enter to add a blank line below the text, and then move the insertion point to the end of the *Drugs* entry.

5. Press Enter, and type the following:

   Three classes of drugs used therapeutically or abused by drug-dependent individuals are associated with stroke.

6. Repeat step 3, and then press Enter to add a blank line.

7. Click the Show 3 button on the Outline Bar to hide the outline's body text. Then to restore the text, click Show All.

   3

Converting Outlines to Documents

We need to get moving on the report, so follow these steps to change the entire outline to normal body text:

1. Press Ctrl+Home to move the insertion point to the top of the outline.

2. Choose Select and then All from the Edit menu to select the entire outline (including the body text), and then click the Body Text button on the Outline Bar. Now the document contains only body text and level one entries.

3. Open the Reveal Codes area, where you can see the codes that control the outline. The easiest way to remove these codes is with the Replace command. Choose Replace from the Edit menu, and then in the Find And Replace Text dialog box, choose Codes from the dialog box's Match menu to display the dialog box shown on the next page.

   Removing codes with the Replace command

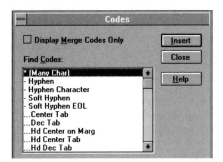

4. Select Outline in the Find Codes list box, click the Insert button to insert that code in the Find edit box, and then click Replace All to replace all Outline codes with nothing.

5. Choose Codes from the Match menu again, select Para Style in the Find Codes list box, click Insert, and then click Close. Now choose Backward from the Direction menu, and click Replace All to move backward through the document replacing the Para Styles codes with nothing.

Replacing backward ⟶

6. Click Close to close the Find And Replace Text dialog box. In the Reveal Codes area, notice that all the outlining codes are gone.

7. Close the Reveal Codes area, click the Close button on the Outline Bar to remove the bar from your screen, and press Delete to remove the blank line from the top of the document.

8. Save STROKE.RPT, which is now a regular document.

Introducing Styles

Just when you think you're getting a firm grasp on Word-Perfect, we throw in yet another feature. This one is called *Styles*. You use the Styles feature to add formatting to specific document elements, such as headings. By assigning styles to these elements, you can maintain consistency throughout your documents. For example, if all first level headings are assigned the *Heading 1* style and you decide to change the formatting for first level headings, you can simply change the *Heading 1* style, and WordPerfect sees to it that all the first level headings are changed accordingly. Because you can make sweeping changes with only a few mouse clicks, you'll find that styles are real time-savers.

Let's assign one of WordPerfect's predefined styles to the title in STROKE.RPT:

1. Move the insertion point to the end of the report's title, and press Enter twice to add some space below the title.

2. Display the Layout Button Bar by right-clicking the current Button Bar and choosing Layout from the QuickMenu. As you'll see, the Layout Button Bar puts many of the features we'll use to format the report at our fingertips.

The Layout Button Bar

3. Move the insertion point back to the report's title, and click the Styles button on the Button Bar to display this dialog box:

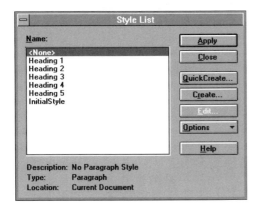

4. Click the *Heading 1* style in the Name list box, and click the Apply button to close the dialog box and apply the selected style to the report's title, as shown here:

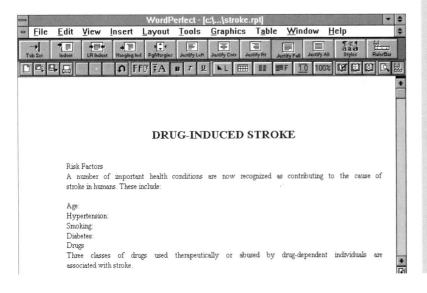

WordPerfect's styles

WordPerfect ships with several predefined styles, called *system styles*, for various elements of a document, including headings, outlines, headers and footers, and footnotes. When you create one of these elements, WordPerfect automatically displays the element in the appropriate system style unless you apply a different one. If you edit the system style, you can restore it to its default definition by selecting Reset from the Options drop-down list in the Style List dialog box.

Notice that Heading 1 now appears in the status bar to the right of the font information.

Let's create a new style for the report's second level headings:

1. Move the insertion point to the *Risk Factors* heading, and click the Styles button on the Button Bar.

2. In the Style List dialog box, click the Create button to display the Styles Editor dialog box:

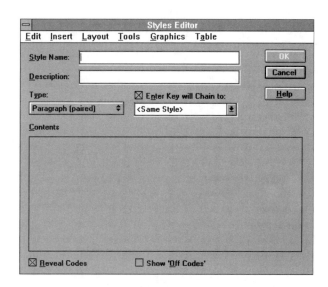

3. Type *Head 2* in the Style Name edit box. (We use the name *Head 2* because *Heading 2* is already assigned to one of WordPerfect's predefined styles.)

4. Type *Second Level Headings* in the Description edit box, and then click the Contents box.

Editing styles

You can edit WordPerfect's system styles or your own styles by selecting the style's name in the Style List dialog box and clicking the Edit button. WordPerfect displays the Styles Editor with the codes for the selected style displayed in the Contents box. You can then modify the codes, clicking OK when you've adjusted the style to your satisfaction.

To format the *Head 2* style, you make selections directly from the Styles Editor's menu bar. Try the following:

1. Choose Font from the Layout menu to display the Font dialog box, and click the Bold option to add bold to the *Head 2* style.

2. Next point to the Relative Size option, hold down the mouse button, and select Large from the pop-up list to add the large size to the *Head 2* style.

3. Click OK to return to the Styles Editor dialog box.

Now before you go any further, you need to define a stopping point for the *Head 2* style; otherwise, when you apply the *Head 2* style, all subsequent text will also be defined with that style. Follow these steps:

1. Click the down arrow to the right of the Enter Key Will Chain To option, and select *<None>* from the drop-down list. Now when you press the Enter key to start a new paragraph, the style will automatically be turned off.

Turning off a style

2. Click OK to return to the Style List dialog box, and then double-click the *Head 2* style to close the Style List dialog box and apply the newly created style to *Risk Factors*.

3. Move the insertion point to the end of the heading, and press Enter to further set the heading off.

Whenever you create a style in WordPerfect, it is automatically added to the Name list in the Style List dialog box so that it is within easy reach. Apply the *Head 2* style to the *Drugs* heading by following these steps:

1. Move the insertion point to *Drugs*, and click the Styles button on the Button Bar to display the list of styles.

2. Double-click the *Head 2* style, create a blank line below the heading to set it off, and then save the report.

The style you just created is available only for this document. You can save the current style list in a separate file so that if you want to use its styles in other WordPerfect documents all you have to do is retrieve the "style file." Here's how to save the list:

1. Click the Styles button on the Button Bar. In the Style List dialog box, click the Options button and click Save As to display this dialog box:

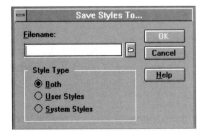

Chaining styles

The Enter Key Will Chain To option in the Styles Editor dialog box lets you set up a series of "chained" styles so that each time you press Enter, WordPerfect automatically applies the next style in the chain. For example, suppose the ordinary paragraph style for a report has a 1/2-inch first-line indent but you want the first paragraph following a heading to have no first-line indent. You can specify that the style for headings should chain to the style for the no-indent paragraph. The no-indent paragraph style should then chain to the style for ordinary first-line indent paragraphs, which should in turn chain to another first-line indent paragraph by means of the <Same Style> setting. With these styles established, pressing Enter after typing a heading automatically starts a paragraph with no indent, and pressing Enter after that paragraph automatically starts the next and subsequent paragraphs with first-line indents.

2. Type *report.sty* in the Filename edit box, and press Enter to save the style list as a file. Click Close to return to the document window.

Using style files

Now if you want to use the REPORT.STY style list for any other WordPerfect document, all you have to do is click Options in the Style List dialog box, select Retrieve, and enter *report.sty* in the Filename edit box of the Retrieve Styles From dialog box.

Our discussion of styles has been necessarily brief; however, you are now armed with enough information to explore this topic further on your own.

Automating Tasks

In the course of carrying out your work, you will often find yourself repeating the same task over and over again. For example, you might have to repeatedly type the same name or phrase, or you might need to format a series of headings with the same attributes. For times like these, WordPerfect offers two features that automate repetitive tasks: Abbreviations and Macros.

Using Abbreviations

Imagine how many times we have typed the word *Word-Perfect* in this book, and think how many keystrokes we would save if we could simply type *wp* instead. Well, we can. With WordPerfect, you can define *abbreviations* for words and phrases you use frequently and then enter the whole word or phrase just by typing the abbreviation. To demonstrate, let's create an abbreviation for the word *stroke*:

1. Position the insertion point after the colon at the end of the *Age* heading.

2. Type a space, and then type

   The incidence of stroke

Creating abbreviations

3. Double-click the word *stroke* to select it, and choose Abbreviations from the Insert menu to display this dialog box:

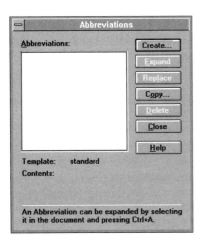

4. Click the Create button to display this Create Abbreviation dialog box:

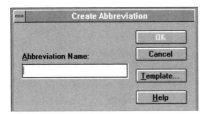

5. Type *s* in the Abbreviation Name edit box, and click OK to close the Create Abbreviation dialog box. Then click Close to close the Abbreviations dialog box.

Follow the steps on the next page to use the abbreviation.

Tables of contents, lists, indexes, cross-references, and tables of authorities

To create a table of contents for your document, start by marking the entries. Choose Table Of Contents from the Tools menu, and select the text you want to include in the table of contents (for example, a heading in a report). On the Table Of Contents Feature Bar, click the Mark button corresponding to the level (from 1 through 5) that you want to assign to the entry. Repeat these steps until all the entries are marked. Then position the insertion point where you want the table of contents to appear (remember to allow enough space for all the marked entries, perhaps including a page break to separate the table of contents from your document), and click the Define button on the Table Of Contents Feature Bar. In the Define Table Of Contents dialog box, specify the number of levels (1 through 5) and their page number positions, and click OK. (You can also change the table of content's style, numbering scheme, and so on in this dialog box.) Finally, click the Generate button on the Table Of Contents Feature Bar, and click OK. Using the List, Index, Cross-Reference, and Table Of Authorities commands on the Tools menu, you can follow this same general procedure to create lists (figures, tables, and so on), indexes, cross-references, and tables of authorities for your documents.

1. Type a space, and continue the paragraph as follows:

   increases dramatically with age. The chances of s

2. With the insertion point immediately to the right of the *s*, press Ctrl+A (for *Abbreviation*) to expand the abbreviation *s* into the full word *stroke*.

3. Now continue the paragraph, pressing Ctrl+A after *s* to insert the word *stroke* where indicated.

   are very small in young individuals. A sharp increase in the risk of stroke *occurs in the population beyond 50 years of age.*

4. Press Enter once to add some space. This is the result:

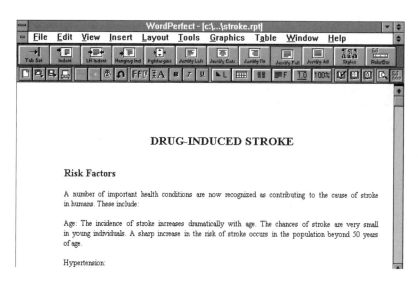

Now all you have to do to insert the word *stroke* anywhere in the report is to repeat step 2 above. This may seem like a trivial example, but imagine the impact on your efficiency if the report included 20 instances of *acetylcholinesterase* or *Rebecca Brand v. Midvalley Clinic*, instead of *stroke*.

5. Enter the following paragraphs after the *Hypertension*, *Smoking*, and *Diabetes* headings to get an idea of the time you can save with abbreviations. Press the Enter key once after each paragraph, and then save the document.

   Hypertension: *The risk of* stroke *increases, as does that of heart disease, in humans who have elevated blood pressure. It has now been demonstrated by clinical trials that control of blood pressure is a major factor in reducing the incidence of*

Using abbreviations in other documents

When you create an abbreviation, it is associated with the template on which the current document is based. If you want to use the abbreviation with documents based on a different template, you can copy the abbreviation to that template by choosing Abbreviation from the Insert menu, clicking the Copy button in the Abbreviations dialog box, selecting the template containing the abbreviation and then selecting the template to which you want to copy the abbreviation.

stroke. *Furthermore, the sooner increased blood pressure is diagnosed and treated, the greater the reduction of* stroke *as well as heart attack.*

Smoking: *Smoking is a well-established risk for* stroke. *The longer an individual has smoked and the more they have smoked, the higher the risk of* stroke *as well as heart attack. It is now known that cessation of smoking at any time, despite the duration of smoking, will significantly reduce the risk of coronary disease and heart attack. Whether the same is true for* stroke *has yet to be demonstrated, but in all likelihood the same will apply.*

Diabetes: *Diabetes and some other chronic illnesses are associated with an increase in the incidence of* stroke. *Diabetics who do not have the other risk factors listed above are less likely to suffer* stroke. *Whether strict control of diabetes itself (maintaining as normal a blood sugar level as possible) reduces the risk of* stroke *is unknown at this time, but long-range clinical studies are in progress.*

Using Macros

WordPerfect *macros* are scripts, or small programs, that automate tasks normally accomplished with a series of mouse clicks or keystrokes. You can create macros that perform all sorts of tasks—from saving and printing a file to opening a new document based on a specific template. You simply give the macro a name, "record" the mouse clicks or keystrokes that you want the macro to duplicate, and then "play back" the macro when you want WordPerfect to perform that particular task.

We don't intend to go into great detail about the capabilities of the Macro feature in this section, but we do want to point out that, with a little imagination, you can use macros to take the drudgery out of tasks such as formatting documents. For this example, we'll create a macro that italicizes headings:

1. Position the insertion point at the beginning of the *Age* heading, and choose Macro and then Record from the Tools menu to display the Record Macro dialog box shown on the next page.

WordPerfect's macros

WordPerfect provides several pre-recorded macros, which you can use to accomplish certain tasks. To run one of the prerecorded macros, choose Macro and then Play from the Tools menu. When the Play Macro dialog box appears, press F4 to display the Select File dialog box with a list of the available macros. At the bottom of this dialog box, Word-Perfect displays a description of the macro highlighted in the list. Select the macro you want to use, click OK to return to the Play Macro dialog box (where the macro's name has been inserted in the Name edit box), and then click Play to run the macro.

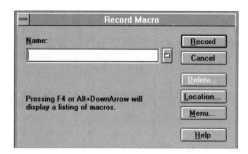

2. Type *i* for the macro name, and click the Record button to begin recording. *Macro Record* appears in dimmed letters in the status bar, and the mouse pointer changes to a circle with a slash through it when it is over the text of the document.

Selecting text with the Find command

3. You want the macro to select and format the third level headings, some of which have more than one word and all of which end with colons. Start by choosing Find from the Edit menu and typing a colon in the Find edit box.

4. Choose Extend Selection from the Find Text dialog box's Action menu to tell WordPerfect to select all the text from the insertion point to the first occurrence of the search string—in this case, the colon at the end of the third level heading.

5. Click Find Next, and then click Close to close the dialog box. WordPerfect has selected the heading.

6. Format the selected heading by clicking the Italic button on the Power Bar.

7. Choose Macro and then Record from the Tools menu to toggle off the command and end the recording session. WordPerfect compiles the macro into a set of reusable instructions.

Now let's play back the macro:

1. Position the insertion point at the beginning of the *Hypertension* heading.

2. Choose Macro and then Play from the Tools menu, type *i* in the Play Macro dialog box's Name edit box, and click Play.

3. Repeat these steps for the five remaining level three headings, and save the report by clicking the Save button. The report now looks like this:

Starting over

If you make a mistake while recording a macro in the document window, you can start over by choosing Macro and then Record from the Tools menu to turn off the recorder. Then choose Macro and Record a second time, enter the name of the original macro, click Record, and when WordPerfect warns you that the macro already exists, click Yes to replace the macro. You can then begin recording the macro again.

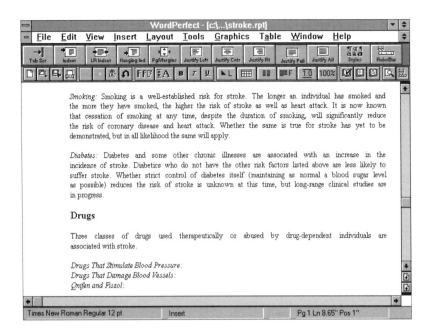

Creating Numbered Lists

If you look at the printouts on page 91, you'll see that the sample report contains a numbered list under the heading *Drugs That Damage Blood Vessels*. Generally, you use numbered lists for step-by-step instructions or sequential processes. WordPerfect 6 for Windows has a Bullets & Numbers feature that makes short work of creating lists, and we'll use this feature to create a bulleted list in the next section. However, we'll use a different technique for the numbered list so that we can show you how to indent paragraphs from both the left and right margins and how to set custom tabs to align items exactly as you want them. Start by typing the paragraph that precedes the numbered list:

1. Click an insertion point anywhere in the *Drugs That Damage Blood Vessels* heading, and press the End key to move the insertion point beyond the Italc code inserted at the end of the heading by the text-formatting macro. (Otherwise, any text you subsequently type will also be italic.)

2. Type a space, and then type the paragraph on the next page. Remember to type an *s* and press Ctrl+A to insert the word *stroke*, and when you've finished, press Enter twice to add a blank line.

Adding comments

To add a comment to a WordPerfect document, choose Comment and then Create from the Insert menu. WordPerfect displays the Comment Feature Bar and a window in which you type your comment. You can click buttons to add your name, the date, or the time to the comment, and click the Close button to return to the document. The comment itself is hidden, but WordPerfect displays a bubble containing quotation marks in the margin adjacent to the line containing the comment. To see the comment, simply click the bubble. Click it again to hide the comment. Comments don't affect your document text when it's printed. (To print your comments as part of the document, choose Comment and then Convert To Text from the Insert menu.)

A few drugs used for long periods of time can damage blood vessels, which weakens their walls and, in the case of arteries in the brain, may lead to stroke. *How these drugs produce this effect is not clear, but it is thought that it occurs in the following steps:*

Double indenting

3. Press the Tab key once, type *1.* (be sure to include the period), and click the LR Indent button on the Button Bar. Then type

With continual administration over long periods of time, the drug accumulates in the cells that line the artery.

and press Enter twice to start the second numbered item.

4. Press Tab, type *2.*, click the LR Indent button, and type

As the drug accumulates, it gradually inhibits the cells' metabolic processes.

Soft page breaks

and then press Enter twice. Don't be alarmed if WordPerfect inserts a soft page break at this point; the position of the page break will change as you edit the text.

5. Press Tab, type *3.*, click the LR Indent button, and type

Eventually, the cells of the artery die, leaving the vessel wall weakened and vulnerable.

Press Enter just once this time. Here's the result:

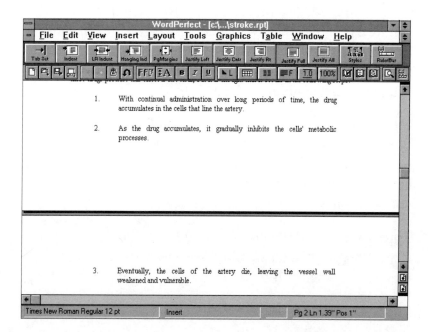

So far, so good. But using the default tab settings produced a rather large space between the numbers and their corresponding text. Let's tighten up this space a bit by setting a custom tab at the beginning of the list. Follow these steps:

1. Place the insertion point just before the 1 in the first numbered list item, and click the Tab Set button on the Button Bar to display this dialog box:

Setting tabs

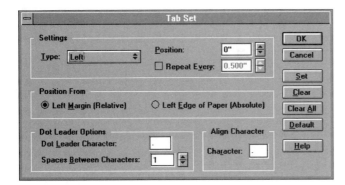

2. In the Settings group box, leave the Type option set to Left, and change the Position setting to *0.75* to set a left-aligned tab three-quarters of an inch from the left margin. Notice that the Left Margin (Relative) option is selected in the Position From group box. Click OK to enter the tab setting and return to the document window. Here's the result:

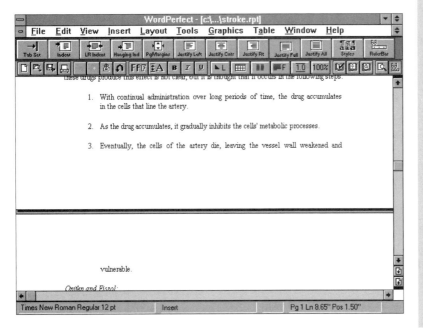

Tab leaders

The four basic types of tabs—Left, Center, Right, and Decimal—are all blank, meaning that the space they control contains no characters. You can set these four types of tabs with leaders, so that WordPerfect fills the space they control with a specified character. The default leader character is a dot, but in the Tab Set dialog box, you can replace the dot in the Dot Leader Character edit box with any character you choose. For example, you might want to use the underscore as the leader character for fill-in lines in forms. You can also change the space between leader characters by adjusting the Spaces Between Characters setting.

Now you must return the tabs to their default settings after the numbered list so that the tab setting at 0.75 inch doesn't affect the rest of the report. This time, we'll use the Ruler Bar:

Turning on the Ruler Bar

1. Move the insertion point to the beginning of the *Qnifen and Fiszol* heading, and click the Ruler Bar button on the Button Bar. WordPerfect's Ruler Bar now spans your screen:

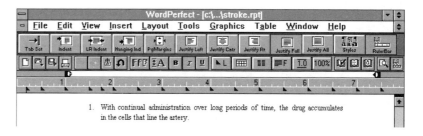

Removing tabs with the Ruler Bar

2. On the Ruler Bar, point to the triangle designating the tab at the 1.75-inch mark (the Ruler Bar measures from the edge of the page and reflects the 1-inch left margin), hold down the mouse button, drag the tab away from the ruler, and release the mouse button. The tab disappears, indicating that only the default half-inch tabs are in effect from the insertion point on.

3. Click the Ruler Bar button on the Button Bar to turn off the Ruler Bar, and then save the report.

Creating Bulleted Lists

If you look back at the report shown at the beginning of the chapter, you'll see a bulleted list near the bottom of the first page. Generally, you use bullets for lists of items that are not sequential or hierarchical. For this example, we'll use WordPerfect's Bullets & Numbers feature, which really simplifies the process. Start by typing the paragraph that precedes the list:

1. Click an insertion point in the *Drugs That Stimulate Blood Pressure* heading, and press End to move the insertion point beyond the Italc code inserted by the macro.

2. Type a space, and then type the following:

   This first class of drugs includes adrenalin, amphetamines, and cocaine. Adrenalin is used therapeutically to raise blood

Other Ruler Bar actions

Above the rule on the Ruler Bar are markers that indicate the positions of the left and right margins and the indents in effect for the current paragraph. You can adjust these elements of the paragraph by dragging the appropriate marker to the left or right. Grabbing hold of the correct marker takes a sure hand, but with a little practice, you'll find that manipulating the margins and indents of your documents with the Ruler Bar is often quicker than working through the equivalent dialog boxes.

pressure, whereas amphetamines and cocaine are commonly abused for their stimulatory effects. The principal actions of all these drugs are:

3. Press Enter twice, and then type the following lines, pressing Enter once after each one:

Increase blood pressure
Increase heart rate
Stimulate brain

4. To turn these three lines into a bulleted list, select all three, and choose Bullets & Numbers from the Insert menu to display this dialog box:

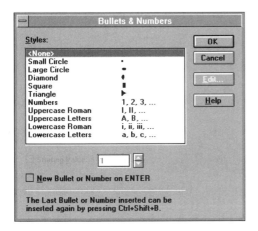

5. As you can see, you have a choice of several bullet styles. For this example, click Square in the Styles list box, and then click OK. Here's the result:

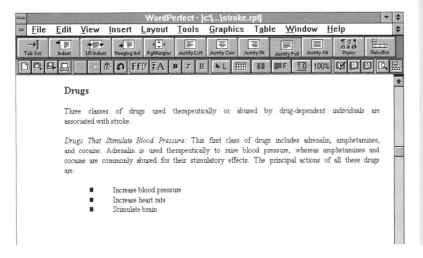

Automatic bullets

Bookmarks and QuickMarks

Use bookmarks and QuickMarks to mark specific places in a document so that you can quickly return to those places during subsequent work sessions. A QuickMark is a generic bookmark that you can go to by simply pressing Ctrl+Q. You can have only one QuickMark in each document. Bookmarks are more work to get to, but you can have several of them in a document. To create a QuickMark, choose Bookmark from the Insert menu, and in the Bookmark dialog box, click the Set Quick-Mark button. Later, jump to the QuickMark by pressing Ctrl+Q. When you set a QuickMark, the existing QuickMark is removed. To create a more stable marker, use a bookmark instead. Choose Bookmark from the Insert menu, click the Create button, assign a name to the bookmark, and then click OK. The Bookmark dialog box lists all the bookmarks you have created. You can select one, and click Go To to move to its location.

Pretty slick! But suppose you want the bulleted list to look more like the numbered list we created earlier. You could manually adjust each item in the list, but here's a quicker way:

Editing the bullet style

1. With the insertion point located in any of the bulleted items, click the Styles button on the Button Bar. WordPerfect displays the Style List dialog box, which now includes a square bullet style.

2. The square bullet style is selected, so click Edit in the Style List dialog box to display the Styles Editor dialog box:

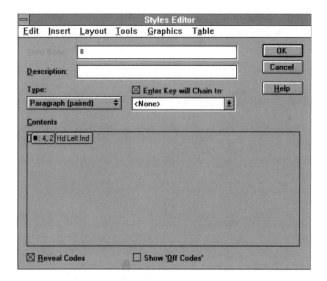

Using other bullet characters

WordPerfect's five bullet styles should meet most needs, but it's easy enough to create custom bullets for those occasions when you want something special. After choosing Bullets & Numbers from the Insert menu, select a style that you use infrequently, and then click the Edit button. In the Styles Editor dialog box, delete the bullet character, and then choose Character from the Insert menu to display the WordPerfect Characters dialog box. Select a character set from the Character Set drop-down list, and then select the character you want from the Characters box. (For example, you can give your bullets more weight by selecting a character such as the pointing hand, ☞ in the Iconic Symbols character set.) Click Insert And Close to return to the Styles Editor, where the code for the character has been inserted in the Contents box, and then complete the editing process as usual.

3. Choose Tab from the bottom of the Styles Editor's Insert menu to insert a Left Tab code in front of the bullet in the Contents box.

4. Click OK to close the Styles Editor dialog box, and then click Close to close the Style List dialog box. In the document window, WordPerfect has adjusted the three bulleted items to reflect the edited style.

5. Now click the Ruler Bar button on the Button Bar, select the three bulleted items, and click a left-aligned tab at the 1.75-inch mark on the Ruler Bar to set a custom tab like the one used for the numbered list. Then turn off the Ruler Bar, and save the report. Here are the results:

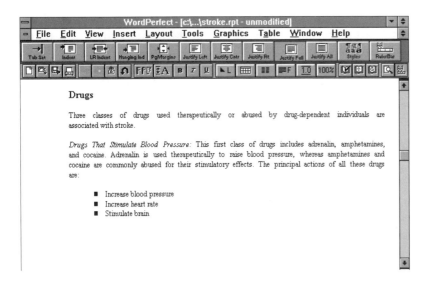

Because you selected the three items before setting the tab, WordPerfect has entered beginning and ending tab codes around the selection, so this time you don't have to worry about resetting the tabs for the rest of the document.

Creating Parallel Columns

In this section, we'll explore ways to use WordPerfect's Columns feature to format information so that it is readily accessible to your report's readers. Here, we'll take a look at parallel columns, which allow you to present unequal columns of information side-by-side. WordPerfect also enables you to create newspaper-style columns, which "snake" from top to bottom and from left to right across the page (see the adjacent tip).

Parallel columns, also called *side-by-side paragraphs*, are useful for creating documents such as inventory descriptions and presentation notes. The easiest way to understand this concept is to look at an example. In the report shown at the beginning of the chapter, parallel columns are used in the middle of the second page to summarize the drugs Qnifen and Fiszol. You cannot use tabs or indents to create parallel columns; you must use WordPerfect's Columns feature.

Start by following the steps on the next page to write a lead-in paragraph for the parallel-column format.

Newspaper columns

To create ordinary newspaper columns in WordPerfect (where the text "snakes" from one column to the next), simply select the number of columns (from 2 to 5) from the Columns Define pop-up list on the Power Bar. To create newspaper columns that will be adjusted so that they are equal in length, display the Columns dialog box, and select the Balanced Newspaper option. You can even insert graphics in your columns to give them that extra-professional look (see Chapter 6 for more information about graphics).

1. Click an insertion point in the *Qnifen and Fiszol* heading, press End, type a space, and then type the following, using the stroke abbreviation:

   Both of these drugs are used to treat osteoporosis (softening of the bone). Both have also been associated with stroke, *but to varying degrees. A summary description of the drugs is given below:*

2. Press Enter twice to insert a blank line and start a new one.

   Now set up the columns, as follows:

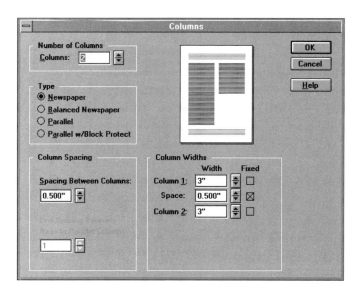

1. Point to the Columns Define button on the Power Bar, hold down the mouse button to display a pop-up list of options, and select Define to display the Columns dialog box:

2. Select the Parallel option in the Type group box, accept the default settings for the other options, and click OK.

   Now you're ready to enter the column text:

1. Type

   Qnifen was the first drug developed for the treatment of osteoporosis. However, after several years of use, it became associated with stroke.

2. Press Ctrl+Enter to move the insertion point to the top of the second column, and type

Instant columns

You can turn normal text into column text with a snap of your fingers. Well, almost. Highlight the existing text, select the Define option from the Columns Define pop-up list on the Power Bar, and specify how you want the columns to appear in the Columns dialog box. Then, to break the text into actual columns, position the insertion point where you want the break to occur, and press Ctrl+Enter.

Fiszol was recently approved for the treatment of osteoporosis. Because Fiszol has a different structure than Qnifen, current theory is that Fiszol will not have the same side effects. However, clinical trials have not yet corroborated this theory.

3. Press Ctrl+Enter. The parallel columns look like this:

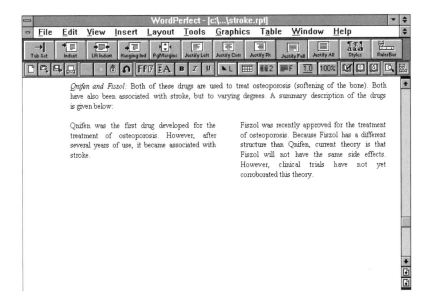

4. Turn off parallel columns by selecting Columns Off from the Columns Define pop-up list on the Power Bar.

5. Save the report by clicking the Save button.

Navigating from column to column is very easy. You can move to the top or bottom of the current column by pressing Alt+Home or Alt+End, and you can move one column to the left or right by pressing Alt+Left Arrow or Alt+Right Arrow. You can edit and format the text in columns just like normal text, including changing margins, justification, and so on. In addition, you can use the options in the Columns dialog box to change the number of columns (you can have up to 24), the space between columns, the line spacing between rows, and the width of columns. You can also add borders and shading to columns by choosing Columns and then Border/Fill from the Layout menu and specifying options in the Column Border dialog box the same way you would specify them in the Paragraph Border dialog box (see page 60).

Navigating in columns

Adding Footnotes

Some reports are more likely to have footnotes than others. If you use information from outside sources or want to steer readers toward data that backs up your arguments, you'll probably want to give credit or bibliographic information in footnotes, rather than cluttering up the body of the report.

In this section, we show you how to create the footnote located on page 2 of the sample report at the beginning of the chapter. This footnote occurs in a paragraph that follows the parallel columns, so start by typing the text of the paragraph:

1. Press Ctrl+End to position the insertion point at the end of the report, and type the following, using the stroke abbreviation where appropriate:

   Although both Qnifen and Fiszol appear to be equally effective in treating osteoporosis, they differ greatly in their chemical structures. While Qnifen contains one methyl group (CH3), Fiszol has none. This structural difference may explain why patients taking Qnifen have a higher incidence of stroke than patients taking Fiszol. The following statement was recently published in the New World Journal of Medicine:

Subscript

2. Press Enter twice to start a new paragraph. (If you want, italicize the journal name and then subscript the 3 in *CH3* by selecting the 3, choosing Font from the Layout menu, and changing the Position option to Subscript.)

3. Click the LR Indent button on the Button Bar to indent the next paragraph—a quotation—from both the left and right margins. Now type the following:

   Early reports of fewer cases of stroke associated with Fiszol would indicate that at this time, Fiszol is a better choice than Qnifen in the treatment of osteoporosis.

4. Save the report by clicking the Save button.

   Now we'll create the footnote:

1. With the insertion point positioned just after the period in the quotation, choose Footnote and then Create from the Insert menu. (To create endnotes, which appear at the end of a

document instead of at the bottom of their respective pages, you would choose Endnote instead.) WordPerfect inserts the footnote reference number 1 at the end of the quotation, draws a line across the bottom of the window, and enters the number of the footnote, ready for you to type its text. It also displays the Footnote Feature Bar, which contains buttons that are useful for working with footnotes.

The Footnote Feature Bar

2. Type the text of the footnote:

R. Urban, "Fiszol versus Qnifen and Stroke." New World Journal of Medicine, 217:312-315, 1993.

3. Next select the entire footnote, choose Font from the Layout menu, select Small as the Relative Size option, and click OK. Here are the results:

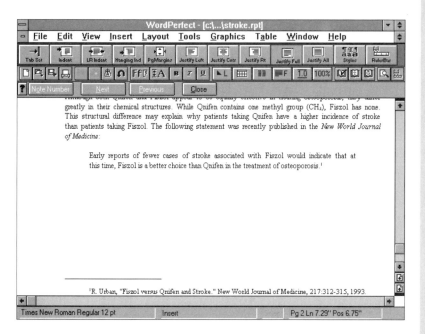

4. Click the Close button on the Footnote Bar to remove the bar from the screen.

You can use this procedure to add footnotes anywhere in your document. For each footnote, WordPerfect inserts a Footnote code. If you insert a new footnote before an existing footnote, WordPerfect renumbers the existing footnote. For example, if you add a footnote to page 1 of the report, WordPerfect changes the number of the footnote you just created to 2. You

Footnote options

You can change the footnote numbers, edit the Footnote style, and access a whole host of other options by choosing Footnote and then Options from the Insert menu. For example, to change the default Arabic numbers to lowercase Roman numbers, select the Lowercase Roman option from the Method pop-up list in the Footnote Options dialog box. To edit WordPerfect's default Footnote style, click the In Text or In Note button in the Edit Numbering Style group box, and make the necessary changes in the Styles Editor dialog box. What about changing the footnote separator line? Simply click the Separator button, and make your changes in the Line Separator dialog box. You can change the line's spacing, position, length, and style; and if you prefer no line at all, just select <None> as the Line Style option. The options in the Footnote Options dialog box also allow you to specify the amount of spacing between consecutive footnotes and whether or not to include a *(continued...)* message for footnotes that are continued on another page.

can delete a footnote by deleting the Footnote code in the Reveal Codes area or by deleting the footnote reference number in the document window. When you delete a footnote, WordPerfect automatically renumbers any remaining footnotes in the document.

When you add a footnote to a document, WordPerfect places the footnote at the bottom of the page on which the reference number occurs and separates the footnote from the main text with a 2-inch line. If the footnote is too long to fit entirely on the page, at least the amount of footnote text specified in the Amount Of Footnote To Keep Together option is retained on the same page as its reference number. If the footnote won't fit, WordPerfect breaks the page, moving both the text containing the reference number and the footnote to the next page.

Adding Page Headers

Take a look at page 2 of the report shown at the beginning of the chapter. This page has a *header* at the top. A header is a line of text containing information, such as a report title, a date, or the name of your company, that you want to appear on the pages of your document. The advantage of using a header is that you create it once and then leave it up to WordPerfect to place it at the top of the pages for you. You can have two different headers on a page, and you can specify on which pages they should appear.

Here's how to create a header for page 2 of the report:

1. Be sure the insertion point is located on the second page. (For the headers to work properly, the insertion point must be located on the page where you want the header to first appear.)

2. Choose Header/Footer from the Layout menu to display this dialog box:

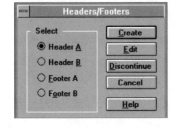

Delaying codes

The Delay Codes feature lets you tell WordPerfect on which pages you want elements such as headers, footers, and page numbers to be printed. For example, you might want to delay printing headers and page numbers on pages that are occupied by large graphics or tables. To use Delay Codes, choose Page and then Delay Codes from the Layout menu, and enter the number of pages you want to skip before the codes go into effect. When you click OK, WordPerfect displays the Define Delayed Codes window, in which you enter the codes using buttons on the Delay Codes Feature Bar. Click Close to return to the document window with the codes delayed for the specified number of pages.

3. With the Header A option selected, click the Create button. WordPerfect closes the dialog box and moves the insertion point to the top of the second page so that you can enter the text of the header. It also displays the Header/Footer Feature Bar, which contains buttons that are useful for working with headers and footers.

The Header/Footer Feature Bar

4. Type *Fox & Associates*. Then choose Line and Flush Right from the Layout menu, and type *Drug-Induced Stroke*. The header looks like this:

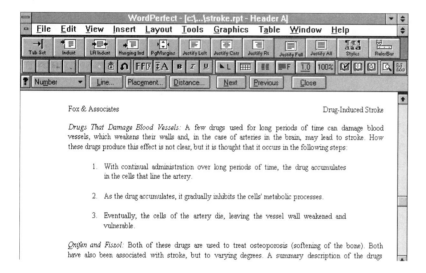

5. Click Close on the Header/Footer Bar to remove the bar from the screen.

6. If you're interested, check out the Header code that Word-Perfect inserted in the Reveal Codes area, and then save the report.

You can change a header by clicking Edit in the Headers/Footers dialog box and then editing the header just as you would edit text in the document window. For practice, let's format the new header:

Editing headers

1. Choose Header/Footer from the Layout menu, and with Header A selected, click the Edit button. The insertion point moves to the beginning of the header.

2. To make the header italic and small, select the entire header, and choose the Font command from the Layout menu. In the Font dialog box, click the Italic check box in the Appearance group box, change the Relative Size option to Small, and then click OK.

3. Click the Close button to remove the Header/Footer Bar, and then click the Save button to save the report before moving on to the next section.

Numbering Pages

WordPerfect's Page Numbering feature is easy to use and efficient. You can print numbers in one of eight different positions on the page and in one of five different numbering schemes—Arabic (1, 2, 3), lowercase letters (a, b, c), uppercase letters (A, B, C), lowercase Roman (i, ii, iii), or uppercase Roman (I, II, III). Follow these steps to number the pages of the report:

1. Move the insertion point to the first page of the report (where you want page numbering to begin).

2. Choose Page and Numbering from the Layout menu to display the Page Numbering dialog box:

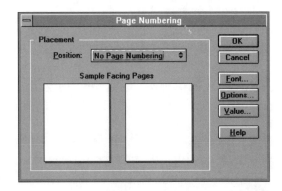

3. Point to the Position option, hold down the mouse button, and select Bottom Center from the pop-up list to print a page number at the bottom center of every page.

4. Next click the Options button to display the Page Numbering Options dialog box, click an insertion point in front of [Pg #]

Line numbering

Line numbers are useful in documents such as legal contracts, where specific lines might need to be referenced. To turn on line numbering, choose Line and then Numbering from the Layout menu, and in the Line Numbering dialog box, click the Turn Line Numbering On check box to select it. Then select a Numbering Method option, and specify the starting number and the interval between numbers (for example, you might display a number for every fifth line). You can specify the number position, whether numbers should start at 1 on each page, and whether blank lines and newspaper columns should be counted.

in the Format And Accompanying Text edit box, and type *Page* and a space. The dialog box now looks like this:

Adding text to page numbers

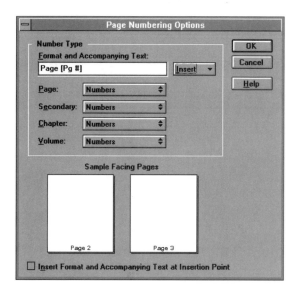

Notice that the sample boxes show *Page 2* and *Page 3*.

5. Click OK to return to the Page Numbering dialog box, and then click the Font button to display the Page Numbering Font dialog box. Change the Size option to Small, and click OK.

Changing the size of page numbers

6. Click OK to return to the document, and save the report.

Turning on page numbers inserts page numbering codes in your document. You can see the codes at the beginning of the report in the Reveal Codes area, and you can check out the numbers themselves by scrolling to the bottom of each page.

Customizing page numbers

In the Page Numbering Options dialog box, you can add secondary page numbers, chapter numbers, and volume numbers to your primary page numbers. (Secondary page numbers are useful if you've made major revisions to a document and you want to keep track of the "old" page numbers. Both the primary and secondary page numbers are incremented automatically.) For example, to number the pages of a multipart report in the format *Part A, Page 1*, you click an insertion point in front of [Pg #] in the Format And Accompanying Text edit box, type *Part* and a space, select Chapter Number from the Insert drop-down list to insert the [Chp #] code, and type a comma, a space, the word *Page*, and another space. Next you change the format of the Chapter option to Uppercase Letters. The sample boxes then show *Part A, Page 2* and *Part A, Page 3*. To number the pages of the next part in the format *Part B, Page 1*, you follow the same procedure, except that at the beginning of the document for Part B, you choose Page and then Numbering from the Layout menu, click the Value button in the Page Numbering dialog box, and set the New Chapter Number option to 2 so that the [Chp #] code inserts B instead of A.

6

Visual Impact

What you will learn

*Import a graphic
and format it
as a logo*

The Fox Report

*Present your data
in an easy-to-
understand table*

DRUG-INDUCED STROKE

Risk Factors

A number of important health
in humans. These include:

Age: The incidence of stroke
in young individuals. A sharp i
of age.

Hypertension: The risk of stro
blood pressure. It has now b
major factor in reducing the i
is diagnosed and treated, the

Smoking: Smoking is a well-es
more they have smoked, the
cessation of smoking at any t
of coronary disease and heart a
but in all likelihood the same

Diabetes: Diabetes and some
of stroke. Diabetics who do no
Whether strict control of di
reduces the risk of stroke is u

Drugs

Three classes of drugs used t
with stroke.

Drugs That Stimulate Blood F
cocaine. Adrenalin is used ther
are commonly abused for the

The following table compares the effects of adrenalin/cocaine, Qnifen, and Fiszol on such factors as
blood pressure, heart rate, and risk of stroke.

Percent Change			
Drug	Adrenalin/Cocaine	Qnifen	Fiszol
Blood Pressure	250.60	25.78	2.30
Heart Rate	5.78	2.70	-3.67
Brain Stimulation	12.00	-34.28	2.46
Bone Structure	0.00	520.80	489.20
Risk of Stroke	2.70	1.56	0.91

PATIENT	GW	SH	BP	PJ	DE	CE	WD	TW	LD	GA	JK	AM
SEX	M	F	F	M	M	M	F	F	F	F	M	M
WEIGHT	178	124	132	198	205	212	156	127	117	167	179	158
BLD PRSS	152	120	145	134	168	136	127	140	128	137	148	143
PULSE	80	63	79	70	90	72	65	85	69	85	74	81
EEG	4	8	9	8	7	5	5	3	7	8	5	4
BONE DEN	23	16	12	31	30	24	17	14	20	10	22	32

*Import a
spreadsheet as
a WordPerfect
table*

The chart to the right is a graphic representation
of the data compiled in the table above. This data
was obtained from a clinical study of 12 adult
patients who are currently undergoing treatment
for osteoporosis.

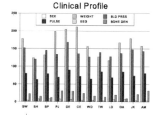

Clinical Profile

*Use WordPerfect
to quickly chart
your table data*

Successful computer applications have to be versatile, and versatility is certainly WordPerfect's strong suit. In fact, strictly speaking, WordPerfect 6 for Windows is no longer just a word processor. You've always been able to use WordPerfect to create tables, but now you can also include formulas and built-in spreadsheet functions in those tables, and you can generate charts based on the tables' data. On the graphics front, you can still import pictures created in other programs, but you can also use WP Draw to create your own images without ever having to leave WordPerfect. In this chapter, we briefly demonstrate how to dress up your documents with tables, charts, and graphics.

Setting Up Tables

Because tables are standard features of reports, presentations, and other business documents, WordPerfect goes to great lengths to make generating tables as painless as possible. You use the Tables feature to specify the number of columns and rows and then leave it to WordPerfect to put the whole thing together.

To demonstrate how easy the process is, we'll show you how to create the table shown at the beginning of the chapter. Start by typing a lead-in paragraph either at the end of the report created in Chapter 5 or in a new document:

1. If you are working in STROKE.RPT, press Ctrl+End to move to the end of the document, press Enter if necessary to add some space, and then press Ctrl+Enter to insert a page break so that the table will be on page 3 of the report.

2. Type the following, and then press Enter twice:

   The following table compares the effects of adrenalin/cocaine, Qnifen, and Fiszol on such factors as blood pressure, heart rate, and risk of stroke.

3. Display the Tables Button Bar by right-clicking the Button Bar and choosing Tables from the QuickMenu.

Now you can start assembling the table:

Quick tables

To create quick tables using the default format, point to the Quick Table button on the Power Bar (the one that looks like a table), and hold down the left mouse button to display a pop-up grid. Drag through the number of columns and rows you want for your table, and release the mouse button. WordPerfect inserts a table with the specified number of rows and columns at the insertion point.

1. First click the Table button on the Button Bar to display this dialog box:

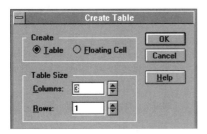

2. Enter *4* for the number of columns and *6* for the number of rows (you can also use the up and down arrows), and then click OK. When you return to the document window, Word-Perfect has inserted a table grid with four columns and six rows at the insertion point, like this:

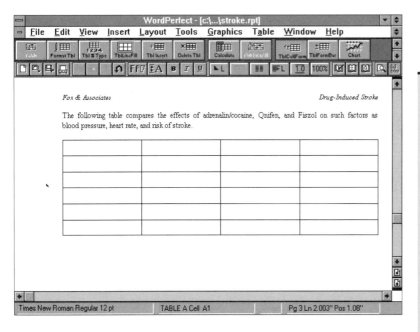

3. Choose Reveal Codes. The Table Def (for *definition*) and Table Off codes tell WordPerfect where the table begins and ends. The Row and Cell codes tell WordPerfect where the rows and cells begin and end. Choose Reveal Codes again to close the Reveal Codes area.

A border surrounds the table, and borders also divide the columns and rows into cells. The indicator *TABLE A Cell A1* is displayed in the status bar, telling you that the insertion

Floating cells

We don't go into detail about *how* to use floating cells in this book, but to give you an idea of *why* you might use them, suppose a mathematical formula in one of your tables calculates the total sales costs for your department, and you cite that total frequently in a report. If the total changes, you have to find and change each reference to the total throughout the report. To avoid mistakes, you can create the references as floating cells that refer to the cell in the table that contains the total. Then if the total changes, the values in the floating cells automatically change. When you have some experience creating tables and using WordPerfect's spreadsheet functions, you might want to explore this feature further.

point is currently located in the cell at the intersection of the first column (column A) and the first row (row 1). Each cell in the table has a similar *address*, allowing you to quickly determine the position of the insertion point by watching the status bar. You enter data in the table as follows:

1. To enter the column headings, type *Percent Change* in cell A1, and then press the Tab key to move to cell B1. Type *Adrenalin/Cocaine*, and then press Tab to move to cell C1. Type *Fiszol*, and press Tab to move to cell D1. Finally, type *Qnifen*, and press Tab to move to cell A2.

Navigating in tables

2. Finish the table by typing the entries shown below, pressing Tab to move from cell to cell. (Pressing Shift+Tab moves the insertion point to the previous cell. You can also use the mouse and the Arrow keys to move around.)

Blood Pressure	*250.6*	*2.3*	*25.78*
Heart Rate	*5.78*	*-3.67*	*2.7*
Brain Stimulation	*12*	*2.46*	*-34.28*
Bone Structure	*0*	*489.2*	*520.8*
Risk of Stroke	*2.7*	*0.91*	*1.56*

3. Now save the document.

Rearranging Tables

You can easily rearrange the columns and rows in a table. Here's how to switch the Qnifen and Fiszol columns:

Selecting cells

1. Point to the top border of the cell containing the *Qnifen* heading, and when the pointer changes to a white arrow, click the mouse button to select the cell.

Moving columns

2. Click the Cut button on the Power Bar. WordPerfect displays this dialog box:

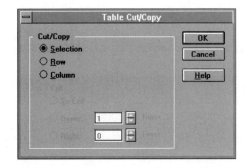

3. Click the Column option, and then click OK. The *Qnifen* column disappears.

4. With the insertion point at the beginning of the *Fiszol* heading, click the Paste button. The *Qnifen* column instantly reappears to the left of the *Fiszol* column:

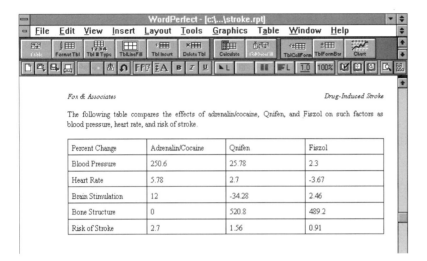

Suppose you decide to use the *Percent Change* column heading as the table's title. The first step is to insert a new row at the top of the table, like this:

1. Click an insertion point in cell A1, and click the Tbl Insert button on the Button Bar to display this dialog box:

Inserting rows

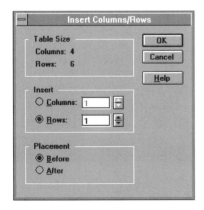

2. With Rows selected in the Insert group box and Before selected in the Placement group box, click OK to insert a new row at the top of the table. The cells have all been renumbered so that the first cell in the new row is cell A1.

Deleting columns or rows

To delete columns or rows from a table, select the column or row, and press the Delete key. In the Delete dialog box, confirm that you want to delete the column or row by clicking OK. (You can also erase the contents of the column or row without deleting the cells themselves.) Clicking the Delete Tbl button on the Tables Button Bar has the same effect.

Let's move the *Percent Change* heading:

Moving cells

1. Click the top border of cell A2, and then use Cut and Paste or Drag And Drop Text (see page 31) to move the heading to cell A1.

Next, we must join the cells of the new row to create one large cell in order to accommodate the *Percent Change* heading. Joining cells is a simple two-step procedure:

Joining cells

1. Point to the top border of cell A1, hold down the left mouse button, and drag across row 1 until all four cells are blocked.

2. Right-click the selected cells, and choose Join Cells from the QuickMenu. The borders separating the columns in the first row disappear, creating one large cell.

Now finish the task by adding a column heading to cell A2:

1. Click cell A2, and type *Drug* as the new column heading. Here are the results:

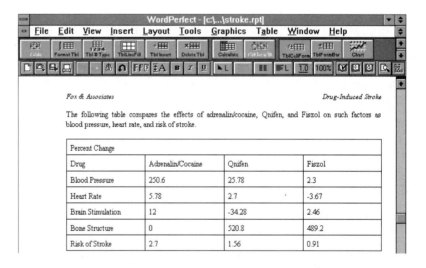

2. Click the Save button to save your work.

Changing Column Width and Row Height

You can adjust the width of any column and the height of any row to suit your needs. Follow these steps to change the widths of some of the columns in the sample table:

1. Right-click cell A2, choose Format from the QuickMenu to display the Format dialog box, and click the Column option at the top of the dialog box to display these settings:

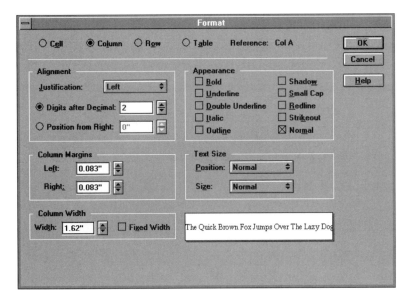

2. In the Column Width group box, type *1.5* in the Width edit box, and click OK.

3. Now try adjusting columns with the mouse. Point to the border between cells C2 and D2, and when the pointer changes to a bar with opposing arrows, hold down the mouse button, and drag to the left. Release the mouse button when column C is about 1 inch wide. Repeat this procedure for column D. (To widen the columns, simply drag to the right.) Here are the results:

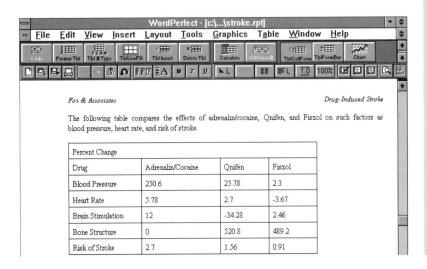

Table functions

WordPerfect provides over 100 functions that make it possible to include complex calculations in your tables. Choose Formula Bar from the Table menu to display the Table Formula Feature Bar. You can enter formulas that perform calculations using values or cell references and the operators + (addition), – (subtraction), * (multiplication), and / (division). For example, you can add the entry in cell C4 to the entry in cell C6 by typing *C4+C6* in the formula edit box and clicking the Check Mark button. To quickly total the values in a range of cells, click an insertion point in a blank cell below the range, and click the Sum button on the Table Formula Bar. WordPerfect enters the total at the insertion point. You can perform more complex calculations using the functions listed in the Table Functions dialog box (click the Functions button to access this dialog box). Select a function from the list, and click the Insert button. WordPerfect inserts the function in the formula edit box with placeholders for the information necessary to carry out the function. You then replace these placeholders with your own data. For example, average the entries in cells B3 through B7 by selecting the AVE(list) function and then replacing *list* with *B3:B7*. The cell entries in these examples must be numeric values, and you must first select the cell where you want the calculation results to appear. Experiment with formulas—you might come up with something like $E=mc^2$.

Adjusting row height

By clicking the Row option in the Format dialog box, you can set the row height to accommodate one line or multiple lines of text. With the Single Line setting, text does not wrap within the cell and pressing Enter moves the insertion point to the next cell. With the Multi Line setting, text does wrap and pressing Enter moves the insertion point to the next line within the cell. You can also select fixed or automatic row height. With the Fixed setting, you enter the height for each row. With the Auto setting, WordPerfect adjusts the height based on the size of the text within the row.

Formatting Tables

Having made all the necessary structural changes to the table, let's add some formatting. We'll format the title and headings and align the number entries on the decimal point. Follow these steps:

1. Click an insertion point in cell A1, and click the Format Tbl button on the Button Bar to display the Format dialog box. As you can see, the settings for the Cell option are displayed by default:

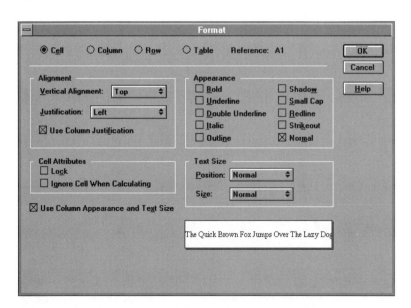

Jumping to a specific cell

To jump quickly to a specific location in a table, press Ctrl+G to display the Go To dialog box. You can specify a Position option that includes a variety of column, row, and cell references, such as Last Cell. Or you can enter a specific cell in a specific table, such as Table A and cell D4. When you click OK, WordPerfect takes you to the specified table and cell.

2. In the Appearance group box, select Bold. Then select Large as the Size setting in the Text Size group box, and select Center as the Justification setting in the Alignment group box. Click OK to return to the document window.

3. Next, make all the headings in the *Drug* column bold. Drag down through cells A2 through A7, and click the Bold button on the Power Bar.

4. To center the headings in cells B2 through D2, select the three headings, click the Format Tbl button, select Center as the Justification setting, and click OK.

5. To decimal-align the numbers, drag through cells B3 through D7, and click the Format Tbl button. In the Format dialog box, select Decimal Align as the Justification setting, and click OK. The table now looks like this:

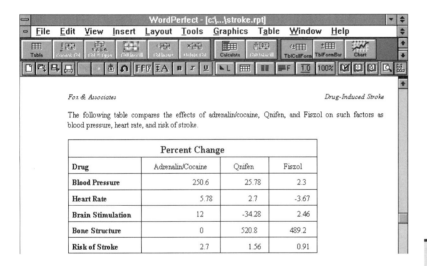

6. The numbers still look a little ragged. To give them all the same number of decimal places, select the cells again, and click the Tbl # Type button on the Button Bar to display this dialog box:

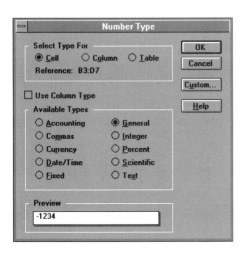

Number types

WordPerfect's number types are fairly self-explanatory and will meet most of your needs. However, for those occasions when you need something special, you can create custom types. For example, to create a Currency type for British pounds, choose Number Type from the Table menu (or click the Tbl # Type button on the Tables Button Bar), and select Currency in the Number Type dialog box. Next click the Custom button, change the Symbol setting to Pound (United Kingdom), and click OK twice. Now any number formatted as Currency will include the pound symbol.

7. Select Fixed in the Available Types group box, and click OK. Here's the result:

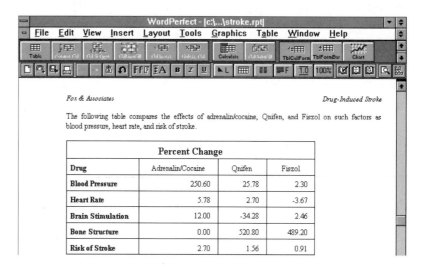

Next, let's change some of the lines in the table:

Formatting grid lines

1. With the insertion point in cell A1, click the TblLineFill button on the Button Bar to display this dialog box:

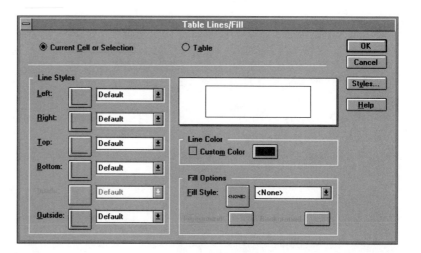

2. You want to change cell A1's bottom border, so click the down arrow to the right of the Bottom option, and select Thick Single.

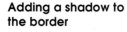

Adding a shadow to the border

3. Click the Table button at the top of the dialog box to display the line and fill options that apply to the entire table:

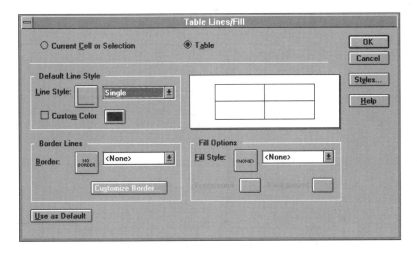

4. In the Border Lines group box, change the Border option to Shadow, and click OK.

The table is currently left-aligned, but it would look better centered. With WordPerfect, you don't have to worry about adjusting margins to center the table on the page. A couple of selections do the trick:

1. Click the Format Tbl button on the Button Bar, and in the Format dialog box, click the Table option to display these settings:

Centering the table

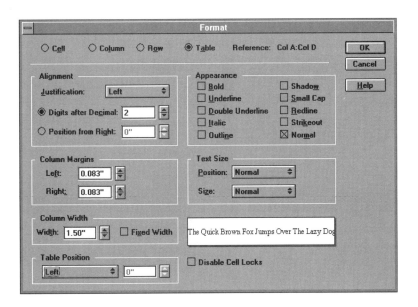

Deleting tables

To delete an entire table from your document, point to one of the table's borders, and when the pointer changes to an arrow, triple-click to select the table. Then press Delete or click the Delete Tbl button on the Tables Button Bar. In the Delete Table dialog box, you can tell Word-Perfect to delete the entire table, the contents but not the structure, or the structure but not the contents. You can also specify that the table should be converted to a merge data file (see page 152).

2. In the Table Position group box, select Center, and then click OK to return to the document window, where the table has been centered between the left and right margins:

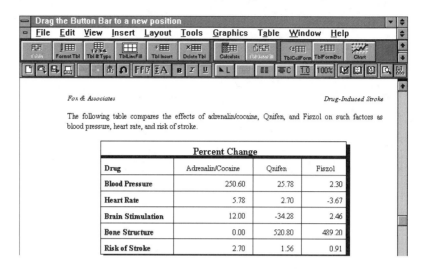

Importing Spreadsheets

WordPerfect's Table feature allows you to create impressive tables and perform a wide range of calculations with ease. But, suppose you have gone to a lot of trouble to create a spreadsheet of data in your favorite spreadsheet program and you now want to include that data in a report. It would be frustrating to have to rekey all that information into a WordPerfect table for presentation. Fortunately, you don't have to. Using WordPerfect's Spreadsheet/Database command, you can import the spreadsheets you've spent hours slaving over directly into your WordPerfect documents.

To demonstrate, we'll pull a spreadsheet that we created with Lotus 1-2-3 Release 2.4 into the report. You can follow these steps with your own spreadsheet file:

1. Press Ctrl+End to move the insertion point below the table, press Enter twice, and choose Spreadsheet/Database and then Import from the Insert menu. This dialog box appears:

Supported spreadsheet formats

Currently, files from the spreadsheet programs listed below can be imported into WordPerfect 6 for Windows documents:

PlanPerfect (3.0 through 5.1)
Lotus 1-2-3 (1A, 2.01, 2.3, 2.4, 3.0, and 3.1)
Excel (2.1, 3.0, and 4.0)
Quattro Pro (3.0 and 4.0)
Quattro Pro for Windows (1.0)
Spreadsheet DIF

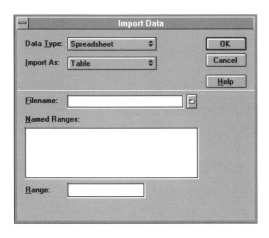

2. In the Filename edit box, type the pathname of the spreadsheet you want to import (we typed *c:\123r24\profile.wk1*).

3. If you don't want to import the entire spreadsheet, type the range of cells that you want to import in the Range edit box, separating the first cell from the last cell in the range by a colon or period (for example, *A1:E6*).

4. To import the spreadsheet as a WordPerfect table, accept the default Import As option, Table, and then click OK. You return to the document window, where the spreadsheet file has been imported as a table at the insertion point. You can then edit and format the table in the document window. For example, we changed the font size, made the headings bold, decreased the width of the columns, and added a shadow border to produce this result:

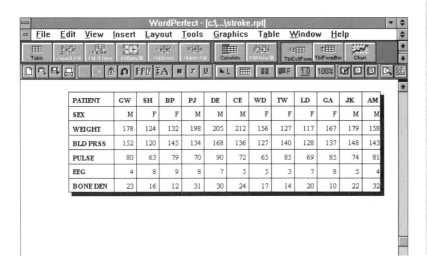

Creating links to spreadsheets

Instead of importing a spreadsheet into a WordPerfect document, you can link it, thereby maintaining a connection with the original data in the source program so that if the spreadsheet changes, the linked copy also changes. To link a spreadsheet, simply choose Spreadsheet/Database and then Create Link from the Insert menu, and follow the procedure for importing a spreadsheet. In your document, WordPerfect displays the linked data as a table enclosed in nonprinting link icons. You can edit the link and update the linked information at any time, and you can delete the link while retaining the spreadsheet data in its present form in your document.

Creating Charts

WordPerfect 6 for Windows now allows you to turn tabular information into a chart without having to call on a spreadsheet or charting program for assistance. As a demonstration, we'll create a column chart based on the Lotus 1-2-3 spreadsheet we just imported, and then we'll add a little text for embellishment. If you haven't imported a spreadsheet, use the WordPerfect table we created at the beginning of the chapter so that you can see how easy it is to generate a chart in WordPerfect.

1. Move the insertion point to the end of the report, just below the spreadsheet table.

2. In the table, select the cells containing the data you want to chart, including the row and column headings to be used as axis and legend labels. Then click the Chart button on the Button Bar. WordPerfect opens this Chart Editor window:

WP Draw - [C:\WPWIN60\WPDOCS\STROKE.RPT in WordPerfect]

		Legend	A	B	C	D	E
Labels		PATIENT	GW	SH	BP	PJ	DE
1		SEX	M	F	F	M	M
2		WEIGHT		178	124	132	198	20!
3		BLD PRSS		152	120	145	134	16!

Title of Chart

| Return | Update | Redraw | CHART EDITOR |

Chart Choose Return to insert chart into client document

Across the top of the window is a grid displaying the selected data. Below the grid is the chart that results when the data is plotted in the default three-dimensional column chart format.

3. Choose Chart Only from the View menu to close the data grid and enlarge the chart area.

Other chart types

You can use the buttons on the Chart Editor Button Bar to change the chart type. Clicking the Gallery button, which spans the top of the Button Bar, displays a dialog box in which you can select a primary chart type: Area, Bar, Hi-Lo, Line, Pie, and Scatter. Double-clicking one of these types displays a gallery of the templates available for the selected type. You can also click one of the six buttons below the Gallery button to select a chart type. The remaining buttons on the Button Bar then reflect the templates available for your primary selection.

4. Choose Layout from the Options menu to display the Layout dialog box:

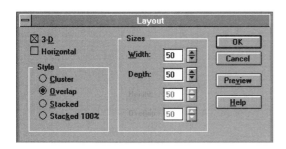

5. Click the 3-D check box to make the chart two-dimensional instead of three-dimensional. Then click Cluster in the Style group box, and change the Width setting in the Sizes group box to 100. Click OK to see these results:

Two dimensional vs. three dimensional

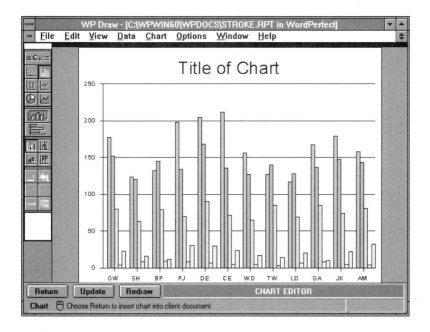

6. Now choose Titles from the Options menu to display this dialog box:

Changing the title

7. Type *Clinical Profile* in the Title edit box, and click OK.

Adding a legend

8. Finally, choose Legend from the Options menu to display this dialog box:

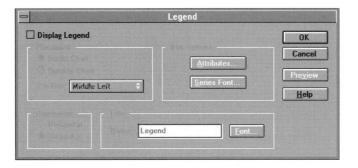

9. Click the Display Legend check box to turn on the legend. Change the Position option to Top Center, and select the Horizontal Orientation option. Select *Legend* in the Name edit box, and press the Delete key. Then click OK.

Having set up the chart, let's insert it in the report:

1. Click the Return button in the bottom-left corner of the Chart Editor, and then click Yes when WP Draw asks whether you want to save changes to the report.

2. For the finishing touches, align the chart with the right edge of the preceding table by dragging it with the mouse. Then you can add some explanatory text to the left of the chart. Here are the results:

Dynamic data

When you create a chart, Word-Perfect maintains a link between the chart and the underlying data. If you make any change to the data, WordPerfect updates the chart accordingly. You can see this relationship most clearly when you have both the chart and the data displayed in the Chart Editor. Make a change to a number in a cell, and then watch as WordPerfect redraws the chart to reflect the change.

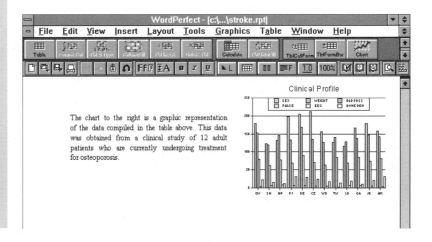

Importing Graphics

Earlier in the chapter, you merged a spreadsheet into the report. The spreadsheet and report document were separate files that, after the merge, became one file. In a similar way, you can merge separate graphics files into your WordPerfect documents.

The WordPerfect 6 for Windows software package includes a number of ready-made graphics files that are suitable for many different types of documents. We'll use one of these files (MEDICAL1.WPG) to demonstrate how easy it is to import graphics with WordPerfect. You may want to speed things up a bit by turning off the Button Bar and Power Bar so that WordPerfect does not have to redraw these elements every time you return to the document window. (Choose their respective commands from the View menu.) Then follow these steps:

Ready-made graphics

1. Press Ctrl+Home to move to the top of the report.

2. Choose Figure from the Graphics menu to display the Insert Image dialog box:

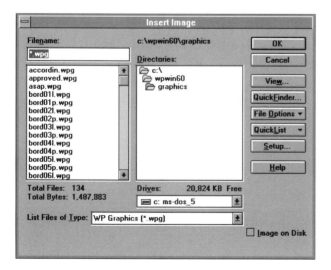

Supported graphics formats

In addition to WordPerfect's WPG format, you can import images in the following formats:

BMP	PCX
CGM	PIC
DRW	PICT
DXF	TGA
EPS	TIFF
HPGL	WMF

3. Scroll to the MEDICAL1.WPG file, and double-click it. Word-Perfect inserts the graphic in the top-right corner of the report's first page and displays the Graphics Box Feature Bar, as shown on the next page.

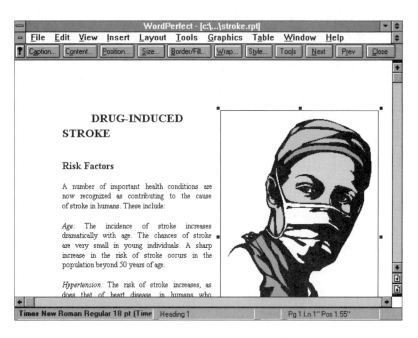

No wisecracks about Dr. Bob! He serves as a good example, and besides, he makes house calls.

Editing Graphics

After you import the graphic, you can change its size, position, and so on to suit your needs. Let's turn the graphic into a small logo. Here's how:

Adjusting the size

1. If necessary, click the graphic to select it. Then scroll the window so that you can move the mouse pointer to the handle in the bottom-left corner of the graphics box. When the pointer changes to a double-headed arrow, hold down the left mouse button, and drag up and to the right to decrease the size of the graphics box. When you release the mouse button, the graphic also decreases in size.

Adjusting the position

2. Move the mouse pointer inside the selected graphics box, and when the pointer changes to a four-headed arrow, hold down the left mouse button, and drag the graphic's "placeholder" (the box with the dashed lines) to the top-left corner of the report. When you release the mouse button, the graphic moves into position, like this:

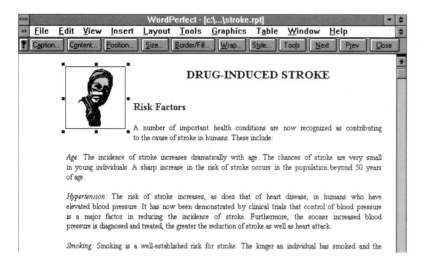

Notice that the text of the report wraps around the graphic. You can adjust the text flow in a variety of ways. We'll do that next, and at the same time, we'll fine-tune the position and size of the graphics box, customize its borders, and add a caption.

1. On the Graphics Box Bar, click Wrap to display the Wrap Text dialog box:

Turning off text wrap

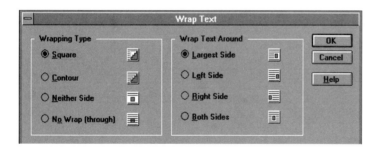

2. Because the graphic is supposed to be a logo, we don't want the text of the report to flow around it, so in the Wrapping Type group box, select Neither Side, and click OK.

3. Next, click the Position button on the Graphics Box Bar to display the dialog box shown on the next page.

Fixing the position on the page

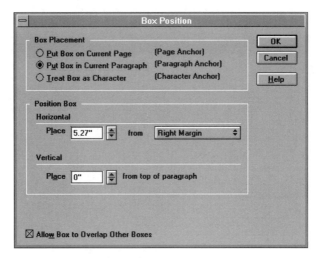

4. To fix the position of the graphic on the page, click the Put Box On Current Page option. Then change the Horizontal Place setting to *1* inch from Left Edge Of Page, change the Vertical Place setting to *0.5* inch from Top Of Page, and click OK.

5. Click the Size button on the Graphics Box Bar to display this dialog box:

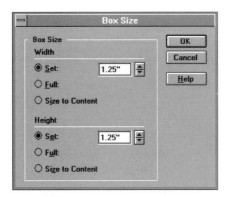

6. Change the Width and Height settings to *1* inch, and click OK.

7. Click the Border/Fill button on the Graphics Box Bar to display the Box Border/Fill Styles dialog box (which is similar to the dialog box on page 60). Select the Shadow Border Style option, and click the Customize Style button to display this dialog box:

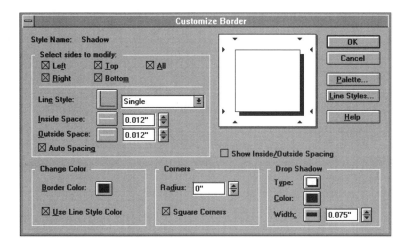

8. In the Drop Shadow group box, click Type, and select the second shadow style. In the Corners group box, change the Radius setting to *1*, and click the Square Corners check box to deselect it. WordPerfect displays a sample border with your selections in place. If you like this effect, click OK twice.

Now we can create the caption for the graphic:

1. Click the Caption button on the Graphics Box Bar to display this dialog box: **Adding a caption**

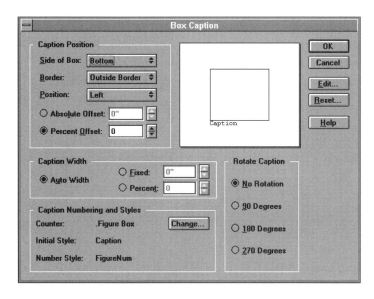

2. Accept all the default settings, and click the Edit button.

3. Back in the document window, press the Backspace key to delete *Figure 1*, and then type *The Fox Report*. Select the

caption, choose Font from the Layout menu, click Italic, set the Relative Size option to Small, and click OK. Then choose Justification and Center from the Layout menu.

4. Click anywhere in the document, click the Close button on the Graphics Box Bar, and save your changes. The logo now looks like this:

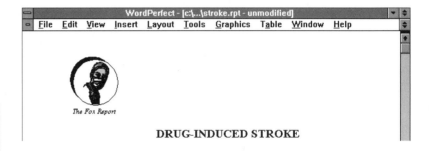

Printing Specific Pages

So far, printing your documents has been pretty straightforward. If you've been working with the sample report, you now have a longer document on your screen that we can use to explore another printing option. Follow these steps:

1. First check the page breaks in Two Page view by choosing Two Page from the View menu. The first two pages of the report should look something like this:

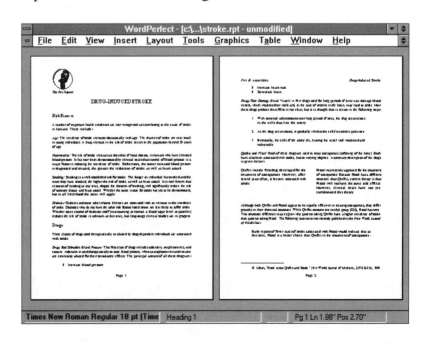

WP Draw

WordPerfect for Windows now comes with a sophisticated drawing program called WP Draw. You can use WP Draw to manipulate graphics from other sources and to create your own graphics. To activate WP Draw, click the Draw button on the Button Bar. WP Draw opens a blank window and displays a palette of drawing tools. As well as drawing straight and curved lines, you can draw freeform objects, circles, ellipses, squares, rectangles, and polygons, and these shapes can be hollow or filled. You can vary the color and style of both the lines and the fill pattern. You can add text in the usual range of fonts and sizes, and you can apply a wide variety of attributes. If you want to get fancy, you can rotate a graphic by choosing Rotate from the Edit menu and then dragging one of the handles in the desired direction. You can even choose Flip Left/Right or Flip Top/Bottom from the Arrange menu to have your graphic do an about-face or stand on its head.

2. If necessary, you can control page breaks so that paragraphs or elements such as lists don't split across pages. In this case, click an insertion point on the blank line before the first bulleted item at the bottom of page 1, and press Enter to move the entire bulleted list to page 2.

Adjusting page breaks

3. Press PgDn a couple of times to check the layout of pages 2 and 3.

4. When everything looks beautiful, choose the Print command from the File menu to display the Print dialog box. In the Print Selection group box, you can select Full Document to print the entire document, Current Page to print only the page on which the insertion point is currently located, or Multiple Pages to print more than one page.

5. Select the Multiple Pages option, and then click the Print button to display the Multiple Pages dialog box:

Multiple Pages

Print Range
Page(s): all
Secondary Page(s):
Chapter(s):
Volume(s):

Print
Cancel
Help

Other printing options

If you've set up secondary pages, chapters, or volumes in the Page Numbering dialog box (see the tip on page 121), you can print the specific pages assigned to those components of your document by specifying the pages in the Multiple Pages dialog box. You can access other printing options by clicking the Options button in the Print dialog box. For example, you can print only the odd and only the even pages (to facilitate copying on both sides of the page when you don't have a copier with a duplex option), and you can print in reverse order (also to facilitate copying on certain types of copiers). If you have created a document summary (see page 77), you can print it by selecting the Print Document Summary option. If you have subdivided your pages (by choosing Page and then Subdivide Page from the Layout menu) and formatted the pages appropriately, you can select Booklet Printing to have Word-Perfect print more than one document page on each sheet of paper in such a way that you can fold the paper to create a booklet.

6. In the Page(s) edit box, type *1*, a space, then *3*, and click Print to print the first and third pages of the report. (To print the second and third pages, you would enter *2-3*.) Your printer responds by producing the pages on which you have placed graphics so that you can admire your work.

By itself, WordPerfect can create some pretty hip documents. Add a few tables and graphics, and you've got awesome documents! WordPerfect's Tables feature makes easy work of displaying your data in readily accessible formats, and its Spreadsheet and Graphics features allow you to tap into valuable outside resources. So be adventurous, and let Word-Perfect help you generate a report that will make your colleagues sit up and take notice.

7

Time-Saving Form Documents

What you will learn

Create form letters for mass mailings using a customer data file

Produce mailing labels from the same customer data file

David Robertson
Sullivan, Duffy and Bridge, Attorneys at Law
145 Salmon Street
Portland, OR 97201

Dear Dave,

I am writing to inform you tha
phone number of our new of

Fox & Associates
Medical Malpractice Consult
1022 SW Vermont Street
Portland, OR 97223
(503) 295-6789

We look forward to contin
Attorneys at Law. Please fee

Thank you,

Kaye E. Fox, Ph.D.

Christopher Dudley
Nesbitt and Gats, Attorneys at Law
3822 Columbia Blvd.
Suite 19
Portland, OR 97221

Dear Chris,

I am writing to inform you that we will be moving to a new location on November 1. The address and
phone number of our new offices will be:

Fox & Associates
Medical Malpractice Consultants
1022 SW Vermont Street
Portland, OR 97223
(503) 295-6789

We look forward to continuing to provide consulting services for Nesbitt and Gats, Attorneys at Law.
Please feel free to contact us at any time during our regular office hours.

Thank you,

Kaye E. Fox, Ph.D.

David Robertson
Sullivan, Duffy and Bridge, Attorneys at Law
145 Salmon Street
Portland, OR 97201

Fox & Associates
Medical Malpractice Consultants
1224 Evergreen Road
Lake Oswego, OR 97035

David Robertson
Sullivan, Duffy and Bridge, Attorneys at Law
145 Salmon Street
Portland, OR 97201

Let WordPerfect take care of positioning the return address

Create letters and envelopes in the same merge operation

I f you need to send the same letter to half a dozen of your clients, you can create a template letter and quickly fill in the name, address, and salutation for each client. But what if you need to send the letter to a hundred clients? And what if you communicate regularly with the same set of clients? Isn't there a way to avoid having to type those names and addresses over and over again?

The time-saver you're looking for is the WordPerfect for Windows Merge feature. You can use Merge to create "personalized" letters and envelopes for mass mailings, as well as a whole host of other documents, such as phone lists, invoices, memos, and contracts. To use the Merge feature properly, you need to be familiar with some jargon, so we'll start with a few definitions, using a form letter as an example. To create a form letter, you need to create a *form file* and a *data file*. Let's talk about the data file first.

The data file

The *data file* contains the information that changes from letter to letter, such as the names and addresses of the recipients. Collectively, the information that will be merged into one letter—in this case, a name, company name, address, and salutation—is referred to as a *record*, and each item within one record is referred to as a *field*. To understand this relationship, take a look at this data file:

Records and fields

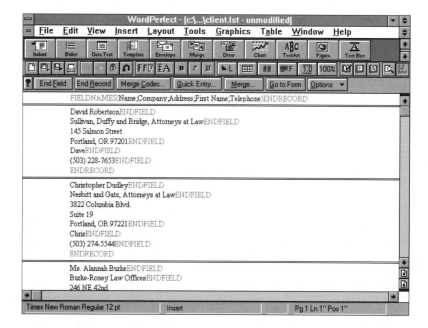

The records are separated by ENDRECORD codes, followed by hard page breaks. The fields within each record are separated by ENDFIELD codes followed by hard returns.

You can include as many records as you want (or as many as disk space permits) in a data file, and you can include as many as 255 fields in each record. However, every record must contain the same number of fields, and every field must either contain the same type of information or be empty. For example, field 5 of every record in the example contains a telephone number. If you have a record with no phone number, field 5 of that record remains empty but still ends with an ENDFIELD code and a hard return.

The *form file* contains the information that does not change from letter to letter—the text of the letter. This file also controls the merging process by means of codes that you insert as placeholders for the information that does change from letter to letter. Here's an example:

The form file

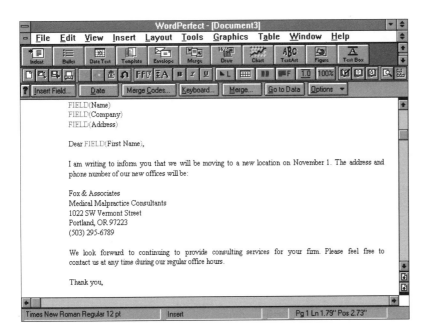

The FIELD(Name) merge code is a placeholder for the information contained in the Name field in the records of the data file, the FIELD(Company) merge code is a placeholder for the information in the Company field, and so on.

Creating Form Letters

Let's create the sample data and form files so that you can see how merging works. Because you will probably use the same data file with more than one form file, you'll usually start by creating the data file, which in this case is a "database" of clients' names and addresses.

Creating the Data File

Each record in the data file we're going to create contains five fields: names in the first field, company names in the second field, addresses in the third field, salutation names in the fourth field, and phone numbers in the fifth field. Fields do not have to contain the same number of characters or even the same number of lines. For example, the Address field in the second record might contain an address that is three lines long, whereas the Address field in the third record might contain an address that is only two lines long.

Starting with a clear screen and the WordPerfect Button Bar and the Power Bar displayed, follow these steps to create the data file, using the sample names and addresses or your own:

1. Click the Merge button on the Button Bar or choose the Merge command from the Tools menu to display this dialog box:

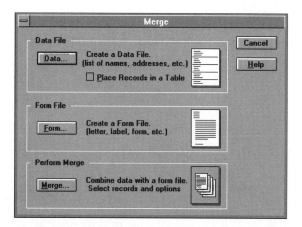

2. Click the Data button to display the Create Merge File dialog box. Be sure the Use File In Active Window option is selected, and then click OK to display the Create Data File dialog box:

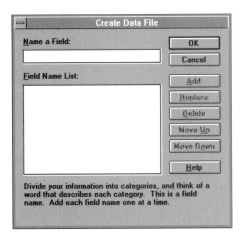

3. In the Name A Field edit box, type *Name*, and then click Add or press Enter to add the first field to the Field Name List box.

4. Now type *Company* in the Name A Field edit box, and click Add or press Enter to add the second field to the Field Name List box. Then do the same for the *Address*, *First Name*, and *Telephone* fields. (If you make a mistake while entering a field name in the Create Data File dialog box, select the field name in the Field Name List box, and then select the appropriate option to replace, delete, or reposition the field name.)

5. Click OK to display this dialog box:

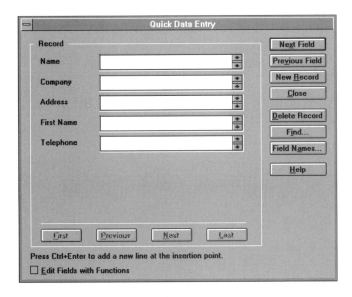

The Quick Data Entry dialog box greatly simplifies the task of constructing the data file's records. (Notice that the five

Editing the data file

You can edit a data file in the Quick Data Entry dialog box. To display the Quick Data Entry dialog box, click the Quick Entry button on the Merge Feature Bar. Then use the options at the bottom of the dialog box to switch between the first, previous, next, and last records in the data file. To delete the current record, click Delete. You can search for a particular record by clicking Find and entering search text in the Find Text dialog box. (Use the options at the top of the dialog box to broaden or narrow your search.) Select the Field Names option to edit, add, or delete field names. When you're finished, click Close. You can also edit a data file directly in the document window using the Merge Feature Bar. Make changes to the records as you would normally, including ENDFIELD and ENDRECORD codes where necessary by clicking the End Field and End Record buttons on the Merge Feature Bar.

fields you just created are all present and accounted for.) Follow these steps:

1. In the Name edit box, type *David Robertson*, and then click the Next Field button to move to the Company edit box.

2. Type *Sullivan, Duffy and Bridge, Attorneys at Law*, and click Next Field to move to the Address edit box.

Fields with more than one line of text →

3. Type the following address in the Address edit box, pressing Ctrl+Enter rather than Enter to start the second line of the address. If the first line disappears while you're typing the second one, don't worry. WordPerfect has just tucked it out of the way for the time being. (To see the first line of the address, click the up arrow at the end of the Address edit box.)

145 Salmon Street
Portland, OR 97201

4. In the First Name edit box, type *Dave*, and in the Telephone edit box, type *(503) 228-7653*.

5. To start a new record, simply click the New Record button, and then enter the following information. Remember to press Ctrl+Enter to start a new line in the same field.

Christopher Dudley<ENDFIELD>
Nesbitt and Gats, Attorneys at Law<ENDFIELD>
3822 Columbia Blvd.
Suite 19
Portland, OR 97221<ENDFIELD>
Chris<ENDFIELD>
(503) 274-5544<ENDFIELD>
<ENDRECORD>

Ms. Alannah Burke<ENDFIELD>
Burke-Roney Law Offices<ENDFIELD>
246 NE 42nd
Seattle, WA 98117<ENDFIELD>
Alannah<ENDFIELD>
(206) 325-9901<ENDFIELD>
<ENDRECORD>

6. After you finish creating the three records of your data file, click Close in the Quick Data Entry dialog box, and when

Data tables

If you prefer to use a table as your data file, choose Merge from the Tools menu, select the Place Records In A Table option, and click Data. If the Create Merge File dialog box appears, select the appropriate option. Then enter the field names (or numbers, if you prefer) in the Create Data File dialog box, and click OK. You can have up to 64 fields, or columns, in a data table. When the Quick Data Entry dialog box appears, fill in the records as you would for a data text file, and then click Close to create the table. You can edit a data table using the Quick Data Entry dialog box as explained in the tip on page 151. You can also edit the data table directly in the document window using the Merge Feature Bar. For example, to add rows (records) or columns (fields), be sure the insertion point is positioned inside the table, and then click the Row or Column button to add or delete a row or column.

WordPerfect asks whether you want to save your changes, click Yes and save the file with the name *client.lst*. When you return to the document window, notice that the Merge Feature Bar has dropped into place below the Power Bar. Your data file should now look like the one on page 148.

Creating the Form File

Now we're ready to create a form file that makes use of the data file's name and address database. Follow these steps:

1. Click the Merge button on the Merge Bar, and then click the Form button in the Merge dialog box.

2. When the Create Merge File dialog box appears, be sure the Use File In Active Window option is selected, and click OK. WordPerfect displays this dialog box:

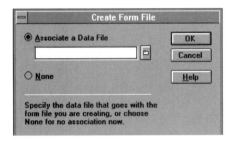

3. To associate the CLIENT.LST data file with the new form file, be sure the Associate A Data File option is selected, and then click the small button with the folder icon to the right of the edit box to display the Select File dialog box:

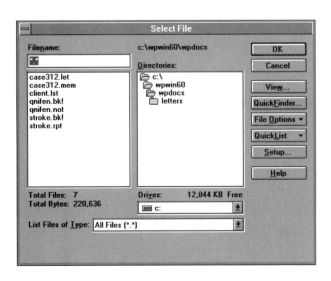

Sorting records

You can use WordPerfect's Sort feature to sort records in your data files. Simply choose Sort from the Tools menu (or click the Options button on the Merge Feature Bar and choose Sort), enter the input and output files, if necessary, and then select the appropriate options, such as which field to sort on, the type of sort (alphabetic or numeric), and the sort order (ascending or descending). Click OK to begin the sorting process. If you want to sort on a specific field, or if you want to sort on more than one field, use the options in the Key Definitions group box. For example, to sort on the second and then third fields in a data file, enter 2 in the first field box, click the Add Key option to add another key definition, and enter 3 in the next field box. You can click the Insert Key option to add another key definition above the current definition or Delete Key to delete the current definition. You can also use operators, such as |, &, =, <, and >, to select specific records with or without sorting the records.

4. Double-click CLIENT.LST, and then back at the Create Form File dialog box, click OK.

Now follow these steps to enter the text of the form letter:

1. Press Enter twice, and type the following:

I am writing to inform you that we will be moving to a new location on November 1. The address and phone number of our new offices will be:

Fox & Associates
Medical Malpractice Consultants
1022 SW Vermont Street
Portland, OR 97223
(503) 295-6789

We look forward to continuing to provide consulting services for your firm. Please feel free to contact us at any time during our regular office hours.

Thank you,

Kaye E. Fox, Ph.D.

2. Press Ctrl+Home to move to the top of the letter where you will insert the placeholder merge codes, and click the Insert Field button on the Merge Bar to display this dialog box:

3. With Name selected, click Insert to insert the FIELD(Name) merge code, and press Enter to start a new line. The dialog box stays open so that you can continue entering merge codes.

4. Select Company, click Insert to insert a FIELD(Company) merge code, press Enter to start a new line, select Address, click Insert to insert a FIELD(Address) merge code, and press Enter twice.

Adding dates and prompts

You can add the current date to your form files by inserting a DATE code. Simply position the insertion point where you want the date to appear, and click the Date button on the Merge Feature Bar. You can also insert a KEYBOARD merge code in your form file so that a prompt requesting additional input from the user is displayed when the merge is performed. To insert a KEYBOARD merge code, position the insertion point in the form file where you want the prompt to appear, click the Keyboard button on the Merge Feature Bar, type a prompt such as *Enter special remarks here*, and then click OK. When you merge the form file with a data file, WordPerfect pauses at each record and displays the prompt so that you can enter additional information. (While the keyboard merge is in progress, you can use the buttons on the Merge Feature Bar to continue on to the next record, skip the next record, and so on.)

5. Type *Dear* followed by a space, and without moving the insertion point, select the First Name field, and click Insert to insert a FIELD(First Name) merge code after the word *Dear*.

6. Click Close to close the dialog box, and type a comma after the FIELD(First Name) merge code. Your form file now looks like the one on page 149.

7. You can use a field more than once in a form file. For example, delete the words *your firm* from the second paragraph, click the Insert Field button, and insert a FIELD(Company) merge code so that the form file looks like this:

Using a field more than once

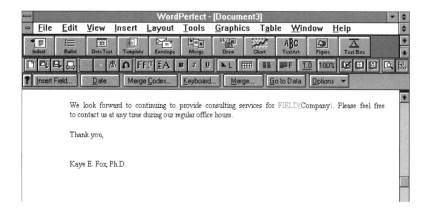

8. Choose Close from the File menu, and save the form file with the name *move.let*.

Merging and Printing Letters and Envelopes

This is the moment of truth. If you have inserted the codes correctly, merging the form and data files will be a piece of cake. And you can create envelopes while you're at it!

1. Click the Merge button on the Merge Bar, and then click the Merge option to display this dialog box:

Merge options

Use the Options button on the Merge Feature Bar to sort data text and table files, print data text files, and display, disguise (as markers), or hide merge codes. You can also tailor your merge by clicking Options in the Perform Merge dialog box. Then, when the Perform Merge Options dialog box is displayed, select the desired options, such as whether to separate the merged documents with page breaks, the number of copies for each record, and whether to leave a blank line for empty fields. (You can also display, disguise, and hide merge codes here.)

Bar codes

You can add POSTNET (Postal Numeric Encoding Technique) bar codes to your envelopes to improve delivery accuracy and reduce postage costs. POSTNET bar codes can be regular five-digit or nine-digit ZIP codes, or they can be eleven-digit DPBCs (Delivery Point Bar Codes). A DPBC consists of a nine-digit ZIP code plus the last two digits of a residence or business number, such as *Kaye E. Fox, Medical Malpractice Consultants, 1224 Evergreen Road, Lake Oswego, OR 97035-5678-24*. To add a bar code to an envelope, choose Envelope from the Layout menu, click Options in the Envelope dialog box, select the Include USPS POSTNET Bar Code option, and click OK. WordPerfect displays a POSTNET Bar Code edit box in the Mailing Addresses group box so that you can enter the ZIP or DPBC code. (If the Mailing Addresses box already contains an address, WordPerfect automatically enters the ZIP code in the POSTNET Bar Code edit box. If you're using a DPBC code, you must still enter the two additional digits.) WordPerfect converts the code to a series of tall and short lines. To add bar codes to regular text, choose Other and then Bar Code from the Insert menu. When the POSTNET Bar Code dialog box appears, enter the bar code digits, and click OK. (This can be handy for envelopes with "see-through" windows.)

2. Because the data file is still open, WordPerfect has entered its path and filename in the Data File edit box. The form file is closed, so type *c:\wpwin60\wpdocs\move.let* in the Form File edit box.

3. Now click the Envelopes button to display the Envelope dialog box, and in the Return Addresses box, type

   Fox & Associates
   Medical Malpractice Consultants
   1224 Evergreen Road
   Lake Oswego, OR 97035

   As you type, WordPerfect enters the return address in the sample envelope at the bottom of the dialog box.

4. Because you want to use the data file addresses, you need to add merge codes to the Mailing Addresses box, just as you did in the form file. Click the Mailing Addresses box, and then click the Field button at the bottom of the dialog box to display the Insert Field Name Or Number dialog box. Select the Name field, click Insert, and press Enter to start a new line. Do the same for the Company and Address fields. The Envelope dialog box should now look like this:

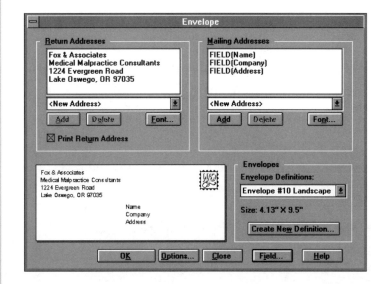

5. Click OK, and in the Perform Merge dialog box, click OK again to begin the merging operation. (You can press Esc or Ctrl+Break at any time to cancel the merge.)

When the merging operation is complete, the document contains the merged letters separated by page breaks, followed by the merged envelopes. Let's take a look:

1. Press Ctrl+Home to move to the top of the first letter:

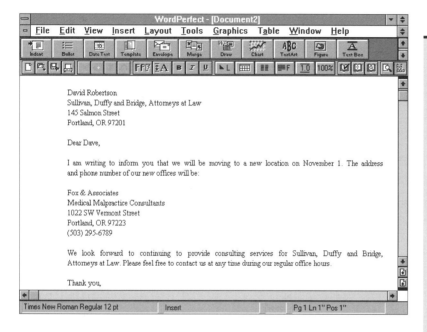

2. Scroll down through the other letters. As you can see, WordPerfect replaced the merge codes in the form file with the names and addresses from the data file to create a "personalized" letter for each record.

3. Now scroll down to the first envelope, and select 75% from the Zoom pop-up list on the Power Bar to get an idea of how the printed envelopes will look:

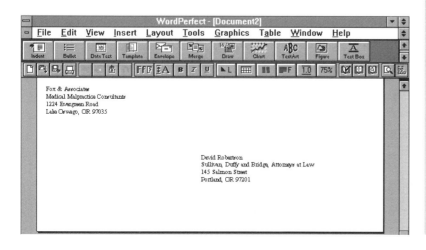

Selective merging

Use the Select Records option at the bottom of the Perform Merge dialog box to select specific records from the data file to merge with the form file. You can then specify certain conditions that the records must meet or mark the records that you want to include in the merge. If you select Specify Conditions, click the Example button on the right side of the Select Records dialog box to see examples of how to enter conditions. If you select Mark Records, WordPerfect presents you with a list of the records in the current data file. To select specific records, simply click the small box to the left of each record in the Record List box. You can change the way records are displayed in this list by selecting options in the Records To Mark group box. For example, change the range of records displayed by clicking the arrows next to the Display Records From and To boxes and then clicking the Update Record List option. To change the display of fields in the Record List box, select a field from the First Field To Display drop-down list, and then click the Update Record List option. Use the Mark All Records and Unmark All Records options to select or deselect all the records in the Record List box.

4. Use the Zoom button to return to 100% Page view. Then click the Save button on the Power Bar, and save the merged file with the name *move.mrg*.

Independent envelopes

Keep in mind that you can create envelopes independently of the merge procedure by using the Envelope button on the Button Bar or the Envelope command on the Layout menu.

Now let's print the merged letters and envelopes. (If your printer does not have an envelope feed and cannot print in landscape mode—perpendicular to the inserted edge of the envelope—you might not be able to print envelopes.)

Printing the merged files

1. Press Ctrl+Home to move to the top of the first letter, and click the Print button on the Power Bar. Because the letters and envelopes are separated by hard page breaks, they print on separate pages. (Be prepared to manually feed envelopes and make any settings required by your printer.)

2. Choose Close from the File menu to clear the window.

Creating Labels

We mentioned earlier that you will often use a data file with more than one form file. To use the CLIENT.LST data file with a form file that produces labels, try this:

1. Click the New button to open a new document, and choose Labels from the Layout menu to display this dialog box:

Canceling printing

To cancel the printing of merged documents (or any document), choose the Print command from the File menu, select the Control option, and in the WordPerfect Print Job dialog box, click Cancel Print Job. You can also press Alt+Tab to display the WP Print Process icon, click the icon once to display the Control menu, and then choose Close.

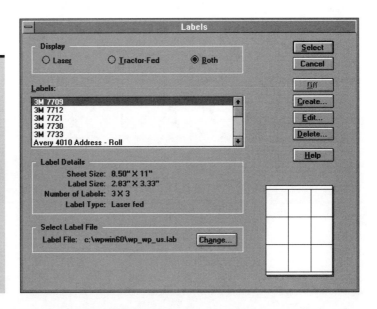

2. WordPerfect enables you to set up labels to print on many types of commercially available label sheets. Scroll through the list of available label formats until you find one that suits your needs. WordPerfect displays the size of the highlighted label format in the Label Details box. A label sample is also displayed in the bottom-right corner of the dialog box.

Selecting a label format

3. With the desired label format highlighted, click Select. (We selected Avery 5260 because our printer can easily handle these sheets of thirty 2.63-inch-by-1-inch labels.) Word-Perfect returns you to the normal document window.

Now all you have to do is add merge codes to the blank label so that it can be merged with the CLIENT.LST data file:

1. Click the Merge button on the Button Bar, and then click the Form button in the Merge dialog box.

2. When the Create Merge File dialog box appears, be sure the Use File In Active Window option is selected, and click OK.

3. In the Create Form File dialog box, click the small button with the folder icon to display the Select File dialog box. Double-click CLIENT.LST to associate the data file with the new form file, and then click OK to return to the document window, where the Merge Bar is displayed.

4. With the insertion point at the top of the label, click the Insert Field button on the Merge Bar. Be sure Name is selected in the Insert Field Name Or Number dialog box, click Insert, and press Enter to start a new line. Then insert Company and press Enter. Finally, insert Address, but this time don't press Enter.

5. Click Close to close the dialog box. Here's the result:

Creating phone lists

You can use the information from a data file, like the one on page 148, to generate a phone list. All you have to do is create a form file with a merge code for the Name field in the data file. Then set a tab around the 3- or 4-inch position, and insert a merge code for the Telephone field in the data file. Finally, press Enter to move the insertion point below the FIELD(Name) merge code, click the Merge Codes button on the Merge Feature Bar, and select PAGEOFF from the Insert Merge Codes dialog box. (The PAGEOFF code will turn off the hard page breaks that Word-Perfect includes in the data file.) Save the new form file, and perform the merge.

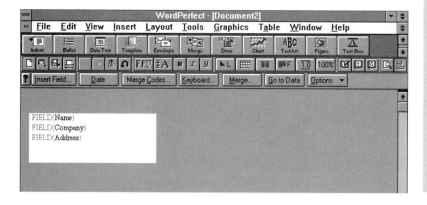

6. Click the Save button on the Power Bar, and save the label form file as *mail.lab* (for *mailing labels*).

Before we actually merge the MAIL.LAB form file with the CLIENT.LST data file, let's add a little formatting. (You can format the labels after the merge, but it's much more efficient to make those changes in the form file.) Follow these steps:

Formatting the labels

1. Move the insertion point to the top of the label, click the Font Size button on the Power Bar, and select a smaller font size, such as 10.

2. Next choose Typesetting and then Advance from the Layout menu, and in the Advance dialog box, select the Down From Insertion Point option, type *0.1* in the Vertical Distance edit box, and click OK to create a little space at the top of the label.

Now let's do some merging:

Merging the labels

1. Click the Merge button on the Merge Bar, and then click the Merge option.

2. In the Perform Merge dialog box, check that *<Current Document>* appears in the Form File edit box and that the correct pathname for CLIENTS.LST appears in the Data File edit box. Click the Reset button to change *All Records; Envelope* to just *All Records*, and then click OK. Here are the results:

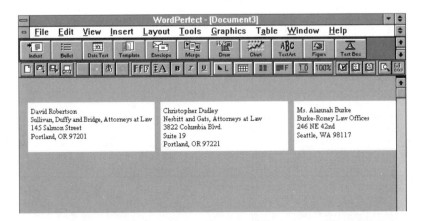

Printing the labels

3. Save the merged labels as *labels.mrg*, and if you happen to have a sheet of the specified label format handy (in this case, Avery 5260), load the sheet into your printer's paper tray and print the labels.

Index